Teacher's Resource

ImpactEnglish

MIKE GOULD (SERIES EDITOR), KIM RICHARDSON, MARY GREEN & JOHN MANNION

Key Stage 3 – Year 8 • Teacher's Resource 1

William Collins' dream of knowledge for all began with the publication of his first book in 1819. A self-educated mill worker, he not only enriched millions of lives, but also founded a flourishing publishing house. Today, staying true to this spirit, Collins books are packed with inspiration, innovation and practical expertise. They place you at the centre of a world of possibility and give you exactly what you need to explore it.

Collins. Do more.

Published by Collins
An imprint of HarperCollins*Publishers*
77–85 Fulham Palace Road
Hammersmith
London
W6 8JB

Browse the complete Collins catalogue at
www.collinseducation.com

© HarperCollins*Publishers* Limited 2005

10 9 8 7 6 5 4 3 2 1

ISBN 0 00 719517 6

Mike Gould, Mary Green, John Mannion and Kim Richardson assert their moral rights to be identified as the authors of this work

All rights reserved. No part of this publication may be reproduced, stored in a retrieval system, or transmitted in any form or by any means, electronic, mechanical, photocopying, recording or otherwise, without the prior written permission of the Publisher or a licence permitting restricted copying in the United Kingdom issued by the Copyright Licensing Agency Ltd., 90 Tottenham Court Road, London W1T 4LP.

British Library Cataloguing in Publication Data

A Catalogue record for this publication is available from the British Library

Acknowledgements

The following permissions to reproduce material are gratefully acknowledged:

Text: Extract from *Dracula* by Bram Stoker, pp9, 11; extract from *Monty Python and the Holy Grail* by Monty Python (Methuen, 1999), p27; Boomerang texts from Rangs Boomerangs at www.rangs.co.uk, used with permission, p29; *The Hook* by Kevin Crossley-Holland, OUP 1998, p38; extract from *The Lord of the Rings* by J. R. R. Tolkien, reprinted by permission of HarperCollins Publishers Ltd © Tolkien 1954, p41; Derren Brown's Tricks of the Mind, an Objective Productions production for Channel 4. Extract from Channel4.com courtesy of Channel 4 Television, p51; extract from *Hurricanes and Tornadoes* by Neil Morris (Ticktock Media 1999), p57; extracts from 'Writing for the Simpsons', from tinyonline.co.uk, pp77, 79; extract from 'The Birth of The Bug' reproduced with permission of Pure Digital, p107; extract from 'Don't believe the hype' by John O'Farrell, *The Independent* Newspaper, 17th February 2000, p111; 'The Verbs in English are a Fright' by R. Lederer from *Crazy English* published by New York Pocket Books 1990 © R. Lederer, p113; extract from *Losing my Virginity: The Autobiography* by Richard Branson (Virgin Books, 2002), p115; extract from 'The True History of the Mary Celeste' by Rachel Wright (Scholastic, 2001), reproduced with permission from Scholastic Ltd, pp125, 127; 'Roman Wall Blues' from 'Collected Poems' by W. H. Auden (Faber and Faber) reproduced with permission from Faber and Faber, p129.

Images: Alasdair Bright, NB Illustration: p121

Whilst every effort has been made both to contact the copyright holders and to give exact credit lines, this has not proved possible in every case.

Printed and bound by Martins the Printers, Berwick-upon-Tweed

Page layout by Ken Vail Graphic Design, Cambridge

Cover design by ABA-design, Ascot

Contents

Introduction		4
Peer Assessment Sheet		6
Unit 1	Gothic horror	8
Unit 2	Tales retold	24
Unit 3	Magic and illusion	40
Unit 4	Destructive nature	56
Unit 5	Family drama	72
Unit 6	Refugees	88
Unit 7	New media	104
Unit 8	Voices from the past	120
Unit 9	Dangerous pursuits	136

Introduction

The following icons are used:

 In pairs   Test watch

 In groups Extra resources

The *Impact English Teacher's Resource* is designed to provide a comprehensive set of resources to aid your teaching, based on the units in the Student Book. In essence, the Teacher's Resource consists of dedicated teaching plans, worksheets, OHTs and assessment materials, designed to help you make an impact on students' learning and progression.

Structure

Each unit in the Student Book consists of three key source texts and an extended Assignment. In the Teacher's Resource we provide:

Source Texts and Tasks

For each of the 27 source texts and sets of activities:
- 2 lesson plans (each with **Starter**, **Introductory work**, **Development** and **Plenary**)
- 2 support resources (OHTs and worksheets.)

These are all cross-referenced to **Framework Objectives** (also referenced in the Student Book).

Extended Assignments

For each of the 9 extended Assignments:
- 1 lesson plan
- 1 planning or support resource (worksheet or OHT)
- 1 OHT showing sample responses at the current and targeted NC levels.

Each of the lesson plans for the Assignments is targeted at one or more of the **Key Stage 3 Assessment Focuses**.

Assessment practice

A full practice test and advice, based on the optional and main English **Key Stage 3 tests** are available to download from www.collinseducation.com.

Using the materials

Whilst you can, of course, use the lesson plans and support materials in their entirety, the resources are designed so that if you choose only to teach one unit or one text from the Student Book you can do so.

The Framework Model

The lesson plans have been devised around the Framework lesson model, and particular care has been taken to make the Plenary session active and meaningful and not simply a recap of what has been taught.

Peer Assessment

A key element of the lesson plans for the Assignment is a Peer Assessment section. In this, the students have the opportunity to measure the drafted work against pre-set criteria and then have their work evaluated using the **Peer Assessment Sheet** on page 6.

Differentiation

For each of the three Student Books for each year, there are individual Teacher's Resources. While the base material is the same, the lesson plans and resources have been significantly adapted and changed to meet the different levels and skills needs of the students. Thus, worksheets and OHTs have different levels of demand, or are, in some cases, entirely different. In a similar way, some Starter activities and Plenaries focus on entirely different areas, appropriate to the students' levels. Finally, the Assignments are designed to move students up different levels so the teaching materials are adapted accordingly.

CDs

All lesson plans and support resources are contained on the accompanying CD-Rom as Word files, so they can be customised further according to the needs of your students.

Interactive whiteboard resources and assessment exercises are also available separately on the *Impact English Whiteboard Resources* CD-Rom.

Finally…

All in all, the *Impact English Teacher's Resource* provides you with a vast range of lesson ideas, support resources, assessment opportunities and back-up. Whether you use it as a flexible, 'dip-in' resource, or as a complete taught programme, it should act as a major stimulus on your students' learning, and assist you with your planning and resource provision.

Peer Assessment Sheet

Date: ....

Name: .... Class: ....

The assignment involved writing a…

Which main text-type features were included in the writing?

What were the good points about the writing?

What needs to be improved?

Writing overview (for you or your teacher to complete)

FOCUS	Poor	Average	Good	V Good
Sentence structure and punctuation (the way your sentences are put together; the accuracy and effect of your use of punctuation)				
Text structure and organisation (the way your writing is organised; for example, whether your paragraphs help the reader to follow what you want to say)				
Composition and effect (the particular choices of words and phrases used to fit the sort of text you are writing) plus how well you interest the reader.				

ImpactEnglish Year 8

Lesson plans and resources

For use with Impact English Year 8 Student Book 1

Gothic horror

Lesson 1

Framework Objectives

W1c: Review, consolidate and secure spelling conventions (word endings)
R14: Recognise the conventions of some common literary forms (Gothic horror)

Main text type: Narrative

Student Book pages 4–9

Starter

- Review the spelling conventions of the suffix '–ful', which is commonly misspelled. Start by asking students for words ending in '–ful' (for example, *careful*, *hopeful*). Remind them that the word 'full' when added to another word becomes '–ful'. Only if the suffix '–ly' is further added (for example, *carefully*) is there a double 'll'.

Introduction

- Read through the extract with the class, checking that students understand the words listed in the glossary.

Key Reading

- Go through the key features of narrative texts as described in the text-type box on page 6. Check understanding by asking students:
  - Explain the term 'narrative', by replacing it with another word.
  - What does the term 'structure' mean when referring to a narrative? (Once clarified, point to its usefulness as a key word when discussing narrative texts.)
- Finally, go over the structure of a narrative (introduction, complication, crisis, resolution) and the examples given for *Dracula*.
- Students answer questions **1** to **4**, which ask them to identify from the extract who the characters are and who is telling the story. Emphasise that the narrative is told in the first person by Mina.

Development

Purpose

- Questions **5** and **6** ask students to consider how the reader is kept involved in the text. For example, we want to find out not only what happens to Dracula but also to the wounded Quincey Morris. Introducing this sub-plot helps to maintain the tension.

Reading for meaning

- Students identify features of Gothic writing by looking closely at an example from the text and then comparing it with an example of non-Gothic rewriting. Begin by discussing the four key features of Gothic writing listed on page 8; point out that these features can be found in a typical Gothic novel. Then ask students to read examples A and B and complete question **7** as a class. Consolidate this work by referring to **OHT 1.1**, which gives annotations highlighting typical Gothic features and those of a non-Gothic rewriting. Using what they have learned, students then complete question **8** in small groups.

Plenary

- Ask students to report back their findings for question **8** (they should identify example C as the Gothic text). Then help them to complete a spidergram on the board, to show some of the Gothic features of example C. Their findings should include the use of exclamation marks, dashes and repetition; ask students how they think these features help to create drama and tension in a Gothic narrative. Also encourage them to pinpoint more difficult features, for example, archaic language ('seeming to bear down upon me'). Refer back to the annotations in **OHT 1.1**, as necessary.

Unit 1 Gothic horror

OHT 1.1: Features of the Gothic style

Extract A below is taken from *Dracula*. Quincey Morris has been badly wounded and Mina is by his side.

The features that are highlighted in the extract heighten the drama. They are typical of Gothic writing.

Extract A

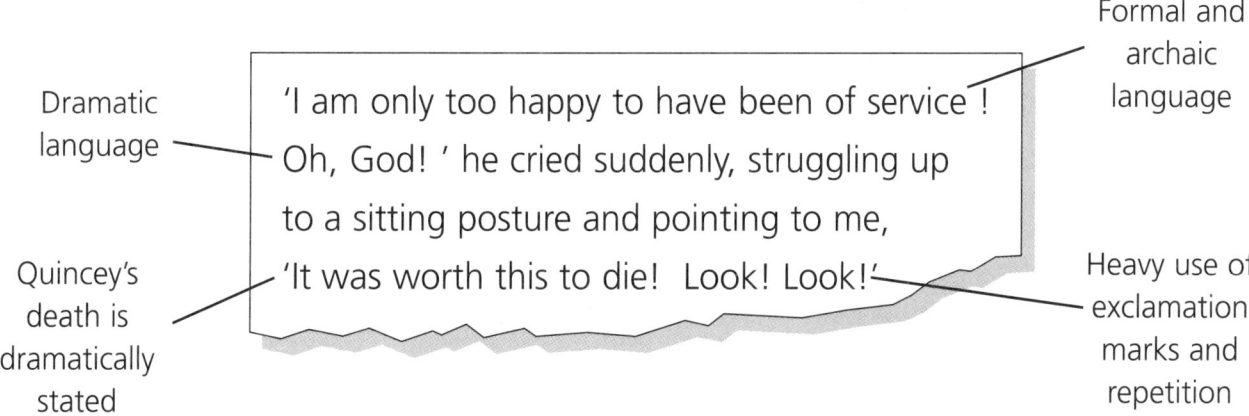

Extract B is a non-Gothic version of the text. The writing style is more low-key, as shown by the features highlighted below.

Extract B

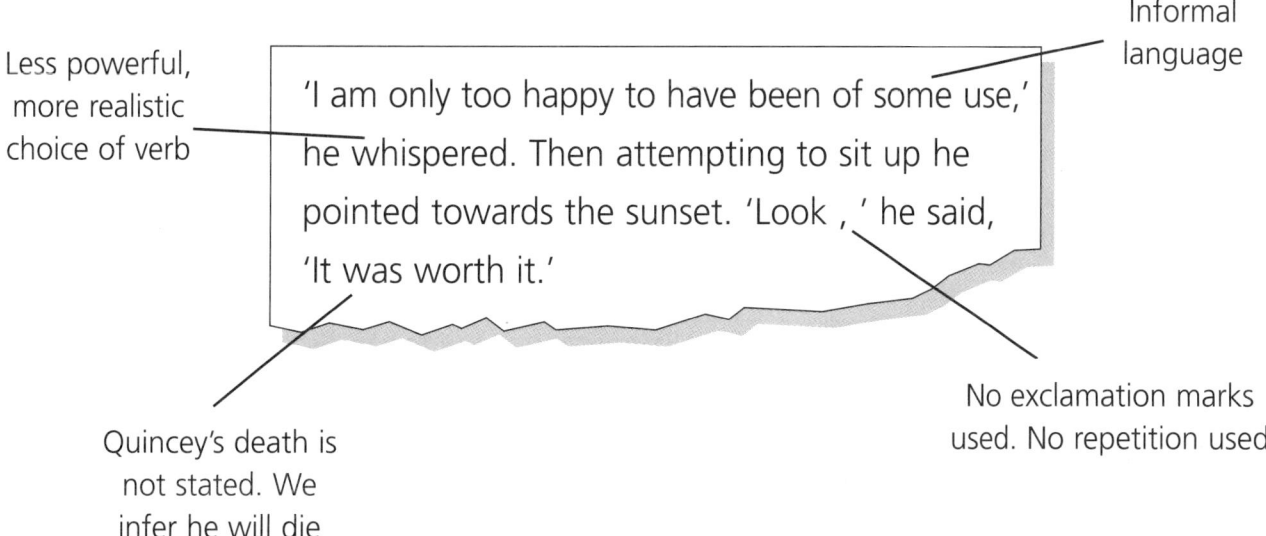

Impact English Teacher's Resource © HarperCollinsPublishers 2005

Unit 1
Gothic horror
Lesson 2

Framework Objective

S7: Develop different ways of linking paragraphs, using a range of strategies to improve cohesion and coherence (choice of connectives)

Main text type: Narrative

Student Book pages 9–10

Starter

- Remind students that paragraphs are a way of organising changes in a text. Point out that they can:
  - show that a new character is speaking
  - indicate a shift of scene or focus
  - represent an introduction and a conclusion.

  Alternatively, a short paragraph can give emphasis to an event.
- Then focus on the way that connectives can link paragraphs temporally in a text, asking students to brainstorm examples of common time connectives (for example, *First…*, *Before…*, *After…*). Record these on the board.

Introduction

Focus on: Linking by time

- Introduce the idea that using certain time connectives at the start of a new paragraph can signal that something is happening at the same time as another event in the text. Refer students to the example given on page 9, and then look at paragraph 2 of the extract (which the given example starts). Ask students to complete question **9** by identifying similar time connectives in paragraphs 3 and 6: 'But on the instant…' (paragraph 3) and 'now' (paragraph 6).
- Return to paragraph 3 and read it through with the class. Encourage students to think about the way in which these connectives add to the tension and drama of the text and do not merely signal events happening simultaneously.
- Give students **Worksheet 1.2**. Read it through with the class, then ask students to decide where paragraphs might start in the text. Working in groups, students annotate the sheet to identify each kind of paragraph; each group should appoint one member to make their annotations. Finally, groups contribute their decisions on paragraph organisation in a short feedback session. Together, the class should decide what types of paragraphs there are and how the text is best organised.

Development

Key Writing

- Before starting the Key Writing task, run through question **10** with students to ensure they understand that both paragraphs denote events happening in time order. Discuss possible ways of continuing the second paragraph and what it might contain. For example, discuss possible sounds the character might hear and what events might follow. This will provide students with a starting point for question **11**.

Plenary

- Draw a simple table on the board with the headings 'Time connectives' and 'Descriptive language'. Students should offer examples of each from their completed paragraphs and record these in the table. Note any particularly evocative or sensationalist language and add further examples.
- Remind students of those connectives that signal several things happening simultaneously and their usefulness in creating tension and pace in a text. Conclude by asking students to outline the function of paragraphs and to give effective examples from their Gothic writing.

Unit 1 Gothic horror

Worksheet 1.2: Making new paragraphs

In the following extract from *Dracula*, Jonathan Harker is staying at the Count's castle and is becoming more and more troubled by events. He decides to leave, but discovers he cannot.

The text contains no paragraphs. However, new paragraphs could begin in several places. Read through the text carefully.

1. Mark where you want to introduce new paragraphs, using the following symbol: //.
2. In the margin, note down why you have chosen to create each new paragraph. For example, because it shows a change of scene.

> With a stately gravity, he with the lamp, preceded down the stairs and along the hall. Suddenly he stopped. 'Hark!' Close at hand came the howling of many wolves. It was almost as if the sound sprang up at the raising of his hand, just as the music of a great orchestra seems to leap under the baton of the conductor. After a pause of a moment, he proceeded, in his stately way, to the door, drew back the ponderous bolts, unhooked the heavy chains, and began to draw it open. To my intense astonishment I saw that it was unlocked. Suspiciously, I looked all around, but could see no key of any kind. As the door began to open, the howling of the wolves without grew louder and angrier. Their red jaws, with champing teeth, and their blunt-clawed feet as they leaped, came in through the opening door. I knew then that to struggle at the moment against the Count was useless. With such allies as these at his command, I could do nothing. But still the door continued slowly to open, and only the Count's body stood in the gap. Suddenly it struck me that this might be the moment and means of my doom; I was to be given to the wolves, and at my own instigation. There was a diabolical wickedness in the idea great enough for the Count, and as the last chance I cried out, 'Shut the door! I shall wait till morning.' And I covered my face with my hands to hide my tears of bitter disappointment.

From *Dracula* by Bram Stroker

Unit 1
Gothic horror
Lesson 3

Framework Objectives

W11: Appreciate the impact of figurative language in texts

R14: Explore how a particular text adheres to or deviates from established conventions (Gothic horror)

Main text type: Poetry

Student Book pages 11–15

Starter

- Although the text in this section is a light-hearted poem, it contains some difficult vocabulary. Remind students that they can often make a rough guess at the meaning of an unknown word by picking up clues from its context. Take an example from the poem and discuss how surrounding words give clues. For example, in the case of 'cadaver', ask students what is likely to emerge 'bloated' from the 'ooze'.

Introduction

- Read the poem to the class. Encourage students to guess the meaning of words they are unfamiliar with, based on their context. Refer students to the glossary only after reading the poem.
- Take time to explain the title of the poem.

Key Reading

- Go over the key features of poetry as described in the text-type box on page 13. Check understanding by asking students:
  - *Give an example of a free verse poem you have read.*
  - *Give an example of a poem with a regular rhythm.*
- Follow this by asking what type of poem *Alternative Endings to an Unwritten Ballad* is (refer back to the title if necessary).
- Discuss questions **1**, **2** and **3** with the class. Students should find a series of regular features in the poem: rhythm, rhyme, verse pattern and repetition of words.

Development

Purpose

- Students can make more than one choice from the list of purposes given in question **4**. The two credible answers are 'to make the reader laugh' and 'to make fun of the Gothic style'. Ask students why the other choices would be difficult to justify.

Reading for meaning

- Help students to build the character of Mrs Ravoon. First, discuss question **5** with the class, exploring what kind of image the name 'Mrs Ravoon' conjures up for them. Ask students why this image is at odds with ideas of the typical Gothic villain.
- Students then search for literal information about Mrs Ravoon in questions **6** and **7**. They will also need to infer and speculate about her character. For example, the word 'cadaver' is described in the glossary as meaning 'corpse', yet Mrs Ravoon is very active. What might students deduce from this?
- For questions **8** and **9**, students complete a spidergram (in groups) before reporting back with a brief written description of Mrs Ravoon. You may also wish to give students **Worksheet 1.3**, which provides a writing frame to support them when writing a full character study of Mrs Ravoon.

Plenary

- Draw up a list of questions on the board asking:
  - what Mrs Ravoon might be
  - how she differs from the conventional Gothic villain
  - what similarities she shares.
- Students can answer the questions by referring to evidence from their character studies. Conclude by asking students to decide as a class what Mrs Ravoon is.

Unit 1 Gothic horror

Worksheet 1.3: Mrs Ravoon

Look again at the spidergram you created for question 8 in your Student Book. What have you found out about Mrs Ravoon?

Use this writing frame to help you write a longer character study.

Mrs Ravoon appears in the poem _____

written by _____

In some ways she is like a Gothic character because…

_____

_____

For example, we are told that she looks like….

_____

_____

Many of the surroundings we find her in are…

_____

_____

For example: _____

_____

But she is also a comic character because…

_____

_____

For example: _____

_____

Her habits tell us that…

_____

_____

To sum up, I would say Mrs Ravoon is like…

_____

_____

Gothic horror

Lesson 4

Framework Objective

W1a: Review, consolidate and secure spelling conventions (vowel choices)
Main text type: Poetry

Student Book pages 15–16

Thesauruses should be available.

Starter

- Ask students to spell the following words from the poem, which contain vowel digraphs: *ooze, lagoon, steer, rune, bloated, baboon, stood, moat*. Then add these words (which are not from the poem): *veer, stoop, gloat, tote*. Students should record any words they do not know. If they keep a spelling bank, give them well-known prompt words as reminders; these can be recorded next to the new vocabulary (for example, *veer – see* [prompt word]).

Introduction

Focus on: Rhyming associations

- Explain to students that part of the poem's success derives from its rhyme, which along with the lumpy rhythm helps to create a comic effect. This is particularly evident in the end rhymes such as 'Ba*boon*' and 'Ra*voon*'. However, point out that those rhymes which contain the 'oo' sound can also have sinister associations with words such as 'tomb', 'doom' and 'gloom'.
- You may also wish to refer students to Tennyson's *The Lady of Shallot* as further evidence of the effect of the rhyme: 'She left the web, she left the loom, / She made three paces thro' the room…'; and later: 'Out flew the web and floated wide; / The mirror crack'd from side to side…', for which further associations include 'died', 'sighed' and 'lied.'
- Mention to students that when we read poetry we may unconsciously make these kinds of associations; poets, too, are not always aware of them. However, by choosing the right words for the poem, other things fall into place. Emphasise this last point when students are completing question **10** (and later, choosing rhymes for their verses in question **12**).

Development

Key Writing

- For question **11**, students work in groups to create their own vampire character. Using a thesaurus, encourage them to find a range of Gothic words. They can record these words on **Worksheet 1.4** and try combining them to see what gives the most successful results. The example given on **Worksheet 1.4** shows how the name in the Student Book was arrived at.
- Once students have settled on a name, they draw a spidergram on which to record key words when creating a setting and character traits for their vampire in question **11c**. Groups then report back, explaining how the words they gathered sparked ideas.
- When writing their verses in question **12**, students, like the narrator of the original poem, should imagine that they are confronted with their vampire character. Remind them to select rhymes from their work in question **10** and follow the bulleted guidance. Point out that in the example given in the Student Book, 'reaches' would be a more appropriate choice of rhyme than 'peaches'.

Plenary

- Ask 2 or 3 students to read their poems to the class. Discuss the different rhythms created and highlight successful rhymes; ask the students to explain how they came up with their ideas. For example, some poems may have begun with a rhyme, others with a particular image. Conclude by asking students what kinds of associations came to mind as they listened to the verses.

Impact English Teacher's Resource © HarperCollinsPublishers 2005

Unit 1 Gothic horror

Worksheet 1.4: What's in a name?

Use this table to organise your work when creating names for your character in question 11.
- List suitable words in column 1. This has been started for you.
- Use column 2 to create a name by combining words.
- Refine your ideas until you create an interesting name, as shown in the example below.

Words	Possible names
death	Demona Death ✗
demise	Demona Demise ✗
demon	Demonica De Mise ✓
plague	
macabre	
gruesome	
morbid	

Impact English Teacher's Resource © HarperCollinsPublishers 2005

Unit 1
Gothic horror
Lesson 5

Framework Objective

R10: Analyse the overall structure of a text to identify how key ideas are developed (through the organisation of the content)

Main text type: Discursive

Student Book pages 17–21

Starter

- Write the word 'argument' on the board and ask students what they understand the term to mean. Then brainstorm for synonyms, to explore its meanings in different contexts (for example, *quarrelling, disagreement, reasoning*). Draw a distinction between the everyday use of 'argument' and its formal meaning. Point out that the original meaning of 'argue' is 'to make clear' or 'to prove'.

Introduction

- Read the article with the class. Afterwards, refer students to any difficult terms in the glossary.

Key Reading

- Remind students of the term 'argument' and then explain the meaning of 'discursive' as 'shifting to and fro between ideas'. Go through the key features of discursive writing as described in the text-type box on page 19. Check understanding by asking students:
  – *Having read the text, what do you understand by the term 'discursive writing'?* (An argument presented from different points of view.)
- Students work carefully in pairs to answer questions **1** to **4**; they should relate their answers to the text-type features, then feed back to the class. In addition, point briefly to the opening statement and conclusion in the article.

Development

Purpose

- Ensure students grasp from question **5** that the main purpose of the text is to discuss whether or not Bram Stoker's character, Dracula, is based on Vlad the Impaler.

Reading for meaning

- Introduce the different ways that arguments can be structured in a discursive text. Help students to answer question **6** by looking closely at the organisation of the article; they should find that it follows structure B.
- Take students systematically through the example in question **7**, showing them how to locate the key words and use the table to make notes. They should work in pairs to complete the table. Finally, conduct a short plenary to see if students have identified the points and evidence for the argument. They can then complete question **8**, completing a similar table to give points and evidence against the argument.
- Working in the same pairs, ask students to complete **Worksheet 1.5**. This will reveal how well they understand the organisation of the discursive text. Topic sentences only are given for each paragraph.

Plenary

- Once they have completed **Worksheet 1.5**, ask students to report back, to ensure they understand how the paragraphs are organised. Discuss the way in which topic sentences have been used, and elicit from students how they knew which subheadings matched which paragraphs. Explain that topic sentences can help when skimming a text to gain an overall impression of how it is organised, as well as giving information as to what the text is about. Conclude by referring back to question **6**, to remind students that this text follows structure B.

Unit 1 Gothic horror

Worksheet 1.5: Organising text

1 There are seven paragraphs in the text *Mad Vlad and Dangerous to Know*. Decide which subheading below matches each paragraph summary and write it next to the paragraph number:
- Arguments for
- Arguments against
- Information about Vlad
- Quotation
- Opening statement
- Conclusion

Paragraph 1 _____

'…his hand grasped mine with a strength that made me wince, an effect which was not lessened by the fact that it seemed as cold as ice…

Paragraph 2 _____

Bram Stoker's creation is as well-known now as it was a hundred years ago, but how many know the origins of the famous Count? Some people think they do…

Paragraph 3 _____

Born in 1431, Vlad, the Romanian Prince of Wallachia, was a ruler of fanatical cruelty. Having seen his father murdered…

Paragraph 4 _____

But how far did Bram Stoker base his vampire on Vlad? There is certainly evidence to suggest that he knew of his existence. In 1890, while on holiday…

Paragraph 5 _____

Those who are convinced that Vlad is Bram Stoker's character point to other evidence: that his idea of driving a stake through his vampire came from…

Paragraph 6 _____

However, it is also possible that beyond the reference to Dracula, Bram Stoker knew little more about Vlad. Elizabeth Miller points out that nowhere in the novel is Vlad referred to…

Paragraph 7 _____

So, is Vlad Dracula and Dracula Vlad? Or is Bram Stoker's creation the work of a fertile imagination with a little help from the Whitby public library? You can decide.

2 Which two paragraphs perform the same job?

Framework Objective

S&L10: Use talk to question, hypothesise, speculate, evaluate, solve problems and develop thinking about complex issues and ideas

Main text type: Discursive

Student Book pages 21–22

Starter

- Help students to recall polysyllabic words by splitting them into syllables. You can also reinforce common suffixes that are often misspelt; for example, the suffix '–ive' could be reinforced in 'dis-curs-*ive*'. Useful key words here might be: *argument, evidence, introduction, conclusion, connective*. (In the last example, split the word as follows: con-nect-ive. Students will find the double 'n' easier to recall.)

Introduction

Focus on: Useful phrases and connectives

- Point out to students how phrases at the start of sentences act as connectives by helping to link views in a discussion. Ensure students understand that the answer to question **9** ('Some have even suggested…' in paragraph 5) serves the same function as the example on page 21.
- Introduce question **10** by discussing how connectives of contrast help the reader to consider opposing ideas. For example: *On the one hand…, On the other hand…* Students then try out a range of these connectives, using examples from the tables they completed for questions **7** and **8**.
- Remind students that other types of connectives also help to link ideas in discursive texts. These include connectives of qualification (for example, *however* and *although*), of sequencing (for example, *finally*) and of comparison (for example, *In the same way…*). Point out how these words and phrases can help students to order their thoughts when weighing up arguments.

Development

Key Speaking and Listening

- Before starting their discussion in question **11**, students should appoint a spokesperson to report their findings to another group. During the discussion, encourage students to extend their thinking through exploratory talk. They should consider which evidence is the most credible and which the least credible. For example, students might accept evidence that suggests the name 'Dracula' was based on Vlad the Impaler, whilst rejecting evidence that the character of Dracula was based on Vlad. Point out that using connectives of qualification and contrast in discussion will help them to think clearly.
- Once students have come to a conclusion, ask each group to complete **Worksheet 1.6**. They will need to appoint a group recorder and agree on what to include in the writing frame. The frame encourages students to focus on the main points and aids the spokesperson when reporting to another group. There are also several useful connectives used, which you may wish to highlight.

Plenary

- Ask each spokesperson to sum up their group's decisions, to see whether there is a consensus among the class. Gather together the main points for and against the argument and list these on the board. Draw up a heading 'New Evidence' and, under two columns headed 'For' and 'Against', ask students what kind of new evidence would be needed to confirm or reject their decisions.

Unit 1 Gothic horror

Worksheet 1.6: Sizing up arguments

During your work for question 11, use the following writing frame to help your group note down the main reasons for its decisions.

In our group we discussed _____

_____

We studied the arguments for and against this.

On the one hand we agreed that _____

_____

This was because _____

_____

On the other hand we disagreed that _____

_____

This was because _____

_____

In addition, we agreed/disagreed with these points _____

_____

_____

The most useful evidence was _____

_____

Whereas the evidence we easily rejected was _____

_____

This was because _____

_____

Finally, we decided that _____

_____

We also thought that _____

_____

Gothic horror

Lesson 7

Assessment Focus

AF3: Organise and present whole texts effectively, sequencing and structuring information, ideas and events

Main text type: Narrative

Student Book pages 23–25

Starter

- Ask students to brainstorm the key features of a Gothic narrative. If necessary, refer students back to the list on page 8 of the Student Book. Help them to think of vocabulary – nouns, adjectives and verbs – to describe Gothic settings, characters and events. List the best of these for students to use later.

Introduction

Stages 1 and 2

- Draw the following diagram of a narrative structure on the board:

   Introduction ⟶ Setting, for example, graveyard, full moon, midnight.
   ⟶ Character
   Complication ⟶
   Crisis ⟶
   Resolution ⟶

- Referring to the prompts in Stages 1 and 2, ask students to choose story settings and use the diagram above to work out their plan for a Gothic narrative. The questions under each stage (on pages 23–24 of the Student Book) should prompt ideas. Allow about ten minutes for this preparation work.
- Next, discuss how students will vary their paragraphs. For example:
  - by using a powerful opening sentence, such as 'The only noise was the screech of an owl…'
  - by including a paragraph indicating a shift of scene; for example, 'On the other side were two graves surrounded by iron railings…'
  - by including a paragraph indicating a time shift; for example, 'After we found the key…'
  - by using a suitable concluding paragraph, such as 'At last it was over…'.
- To reinforce different paragraph types, give out **Worksheet 1.7**. This asks students to identify different types of paragraph from a series of paragraph openers.

Development

Stage 3

- Students write their Gothic stories, using their plans from Stages 1 and 2 and varying their paragraphs. They should write in the first person and the present tense, and draw on the list of vocabulary created during the Starter.

Challenge

- Here students are asked to look at the descriptive language they used in their stories. Encourage them to use dramatic words or phrases to make their writing more Gothic in style.

Impact English Teacher's Resource © HarperCollinsPublishers 2005

Peer Assessment

- When students have completed their writing, they should read each others' drafts in pairs. Write up the text-type features listed below and ask students to check whether their drafts include them:
  - narrative structure
  - powerful opening sentence
  - work is organised in paragraphs
  - use of first person
  - use of past tense.
- Students then fill in the Peer Assessment Sheet (see page 6) and feed back their findings to the class.
- Students redraft according to suggestions.

Plenary

- Give a copy of **OHT 1.8** (top half only) to groups of students and ask them to annotate the level 3 writing to show how well the student has incorporated the various features of good narrative writing, and what needs improvement. Then display the whole of **OHT 1.8** and ask for feedback on how to get the level 3 writing up to level 4. Show in the exemplar of level 4 how this can be done. Students can make changes to their own texts in light of this.

Unit 1 Gothic horror

Worksheet 1.7: Paragraph types

The following starter paragraphs could all come from one story.

1 Identify what kind of paragraphs they are. Choose from the following:
A: opening
B: conclusion
C: shift of scene
D: shift of time
E: direct speech.
Write the correct letter beside each paragraph.

2 Underline any words (such as connectives) that give you clues as to what type of paragraph they are.

Paragraph 1 _____

On the other side were two graves surrounded by iron railings.

Paragraph 2 _____

We raced down the cemetery path and scrambled over the wall, just as the sun was creeping above the horizon. We were safe.

Paragraph 3 _____

A moment later there was a deafening howl and a strange shape appeared from behind the tree.

Paragraph 4 _____

I pulled up my hood as I slipped out of the front door, quietly closing it behind me. What strange events lay ahead?

Paragraph 4 _____

'Come quickly!' Jack called to me urgently.

Paragraph 5 _____

We ran towards the open fields and threw ourselves down on the grass, out of breath, grateful for a few moments to recover…

Unit 1 — Gothic horror

OHT 1.8: Raising the level

Assessment Focus

AF3: Organise and present whole texts effectively, sequencing and structuring information, ideas and events

Level 3

I climbed over the gates as quickly as I could and walked towards the disused fairground. It was on the far side of the park near a small wood. As I passed the café I could see the shutters were down. It was closed for the winter. Then I stopped. In the far distance I heard the sound of a merry-go-round.

Level 4

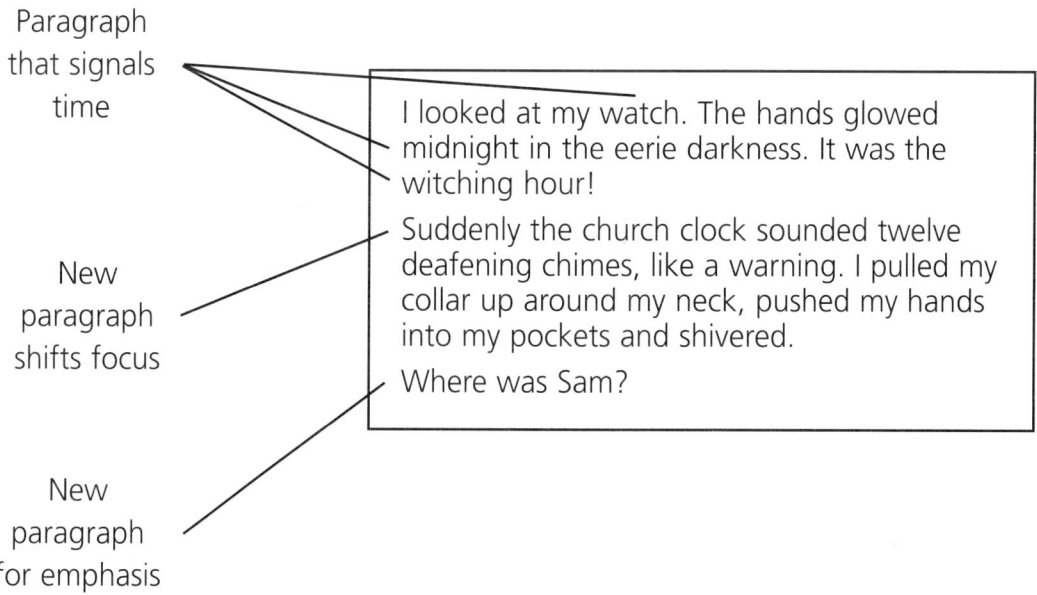

Paragraph that signals time →

I looked at my watch. The hands glowed midnight in the eerie darkness. It was the witching hour!

New paragraph shifts focus →

Suddenly the church clock sounded twelve deafening chimes, like a warning. I pulled my collar up around my neck, pushed my hands into my pockets and shivered.

New paragraph for emphasis →

Where was Sam?

Tales retold

Lesson

Framework Objective

S12: Explore and use different degrees of formality in written and oral texts

Main text type: Narrative

Student Book pages 26–30

Starter

- Ask the class what the difference is between formal and informal language, and explain, if necessary, that formal language follows the strict rules of standard english in vocabulary, structure, grammar and spelling; whereas informal language is more loosely structured and sometimes ignores grammatical rules and includes slang and colloquialisms. Give pairs a set of the cards on **Worksheet 2.1** and get them to group the words and phrases into formal and informal sections.

Introduction

- Read through the extract with the class and check that difficult words are understood. Ask 1 or 2 students what the story is about.

Key Reading

- Go through the key features of narrative texts as shown in the text-type box on page 28. Check understanding by asking students:
  - *What is a crisis? Give some examples from books you have recently read.*
  - *What is the difference between a first-person narrative and a third-person narrative?*
  - *What other text types often use expressive and descriptive language?*
  - *How does the writer indicate the words spoken in direct speech?*
- Students discuss questions **1** to **6** in pairs. Less able students may need guidance for question **6** in deducing which character is speaking. Invite 2 or 3 pairs to feed back their answers and invite the class to comment.

Development

Purpose

- Students discuss question **7** in small groups and feed back. All of the answers except the first could be argued for successfully.

Reading for meaning

- Students answer questions **8** to **12**, which look at different stylistic effects, on their own or in pairs and then feed back.
- As a context for question **12**, you may like to read out or display a version of the original Greek myth, to show the formal language and serious tone (try the version found at www.bulfinch.org/fables/bull16.html#sphinx). You may also need to remind the class of the difference between formal and informal language (refer back to the Starter activity).

Plenary

- Ask students to summarise the three most important things they have learned in this lesson by presenting them as a series of bullet points. Then invite 2 or 3 students to feed back and try to gain class consensus on the top three points.

Unit 2 Tales retold

Worksheet 2.1: Formal or informal

Informal	Formal
Off his head	A splendid achievement
Give me a break	Yours sincerely
Give us a kiss	Can you not see?
That's cool	The conclusion is that…
I'm, like, sitting there…	Appropriate to the situation
No, I can't	
Getting the hang of it	
How ya doin?	
That's right	

Tales retold

Lesson 2

Framework Objectives

Wr6: Experiment with figurative language in conveying a sense of character and setting

Wr8: Develop an imaginative or unusual treatment of familiar material or established conventions

Main text type: Narrative

Student Book pages 31–32

Starter

- Show **OHT 2.2** to the class (or, even better, show them the clip from *Monty Python and the Holy Grail*) and discuss how it creates a humorous effect. In particular, ask students:
  - *What traditional tale or tales are being made fun of here?* (King Arthur and the riddle theme, combined with the traveller at the gates/bridge theme.)
  - *What features of the text relate to a serious, ancient tale?*
  - *What features are deliberately different?*
  - *What creates the humour?*
- Relate this example to the humorous take on the Sphinx tale in the extract they have been working on.

Introduction

Focus on: Similes

- Read through the section, showing the main ingredients of the sample simile. Ask students what the simile adds to the description. For example, the author could have written: *My bristles stood on end with fright.* Question **13** elicits the effect of this simile, while question **14** supplies four sentences to turn into similes. Students could discuss these in pairs before writing their answers (as complete sentences) in their books. Get students to read out their sentences and invite the class to comment on how effective they are.

Development

Key Writing

- In the Greek myth, the Sphinx asked passers-by this riddle: 'What creature walks on four legs in the morning, two in the afternoon and three in the evening?' Ask the class the same riddle and get them to discuss it. The answer is Man – in the 'morning' of life he crawls (as a baby); in the 'afternoon' (adulthood) he walks; in the 'evening' (old age) he walks with a stick. You could also point out the metaphors here.
- Next, explain the writing task (question **15**) to students, in which they are going to add humour to the story of Gryllus and Sibyl by including references to a TV game show. Draw up the spidergram with the class if support is necessary. Pairs decide on one or two features from the spidergram to include in their episode, then role-play a dialogue. Afterwards, bring the class together and invite pairs to discuss any ideas they have come up with. Or ask 1 or 2 pairs to role-play in front of the class.
- Allow plenty of time for students to draft the episode. Work with a group to share ideas, give positive criticism and praise achievement. Encourage students to include a simile in their narrative. Some students may want to use comic ideas from the Monty Python script discussed in the Starter (on **OHT 2.2**).

Plenary

- Invite 3 or 4 pairs to read out their game show narratives and invite the rest of the class to comment on how effective they are. Have students managed to refer both to the world of ancient myth and the modern world of the game show?
- To conclude, you may like to read the class Paul Shipton's continuation of the story and ask students to comment on how effective it is.

Unit 2 Tales retold

OHT 2.2: Monty Python

BRIDGEKEEPER: Stop! Who would cross the Bridge of Death must answer me these questions three, ere the other side he see.
LAUNCELOT: Ask me the questions, bridgekeeper. I am not afraid.
BRIDGEKEEPER: What is your name?
LAUNCELOT: My name is Sir Launcelot of Camelot.
BRIDGEKEEPER: What is your quest?
LAUNCELOT: To seek the Holy Grail.
BRIDGEKEEPER: What is your favourite colour?
LAUNCELOT: Blue.
BRIDGEKEEPER: Right. Off you go.
LAUNCELOT: Oh, thank you. Thank you very much.
ROBIN: That's easy!
BRIDGEKEEPER: Stop! Who approacheth the Bridge of Death must answer me these questions three, ere the other side he see.
ROBIN: Ask me the questions, bridgekeeper. I'm not afraid.
BRIDGEKEEPER: What is your name?
ROBIN: Sir Robin of Camelot.
BRIDGEKEEPER: What is your quest?
ROBIN: To seek the Holy Grail.
BRIDGEKEEPER: What is the capital of Assyria?
ROBIN: I don't know that! Auuuuuuuugh!
[ROBIN explodes and dies]
BRIDGEKEEPER: Stop! What is your name?
GALAHAD: Sir Galahad of Camelot.
BRIDGEKEEPER: What is your quest?
GALAHAD: I seek the Grail.
BRIDGEKEEPER: What is your favourite colour?
GALAHAD: Blue. No yel– auuuuuuuugh!
[GALAHAD explodes and dies]
BRIDGEKEEPER: Hee hee heh. Stop! What is your name?
ARTHUR: It is Arthur, King of the Britons.
BRIDGEKEEPER: What is your quest?
ARTHUR: To seek the Holy Grail.
BRIDGEKEEPER: What is the air-speed velocity of an unladen swallow?
ARTHUR: What do you mean? An African or European swallow?
BRIDGEKEEPER: Huh? I—I don't know that! Auuuuuuuugh!
[BRIDGEKEEPER explodes and dies]
BEDEVERE: How do know so much about swallows?
ARTHUR: Well, you have to know these things when you're a king, you know.

From *Monty Python and the Holy Grail*

Urban legends

Tales retold

Lesson  3

Framework Objective

R4: Review their developing skills as active, critical readers who search for meaning using a range of reading strategies

Main text type: Explanation

Student Book pages 33–37

Starter

- Without students opening their books, read out the urban legend on page 33 of the Student Book (or tell another one that you know). Ask students what kind of story it is – elicit the term 'urban legend' or 'urban myth'. Get students in groups to share any urban legends they know and work out their own definition of an urban legend. Share group definitions as a class.

Introduction

- Read the website text with the class, and check that difficult words are understood. Ask students what the text is about.

Key Reading

- Go through the key features of explanation texts as shown in the text-type box on page 35. Check understanding by asking students:
  - *Why are explanation texts written in clear and logical steps?*
  - *What does 'causal language' mean?*
  - *Give an example of formal language.*
- Students discuss questions **1**, **2** and **3** in pairs, then feed back with their answers. Be ready to provide further examples of causal language to support question **2**.

Development

Purpose

- Students work in small groups to answer questions **4** and **5**. Ask 2 or 3 groups to feed back their answers and invite the class to comment. If necessary, during question **5b** prompt students as to why a story has been included; for example, as an example to give the explanation a context.

Reading for meaning

- Students can discuss questions **6** to **9** in pairs or work on them individually, before feeding back to the class. Before they tackle question **9**, run through the 'Grammar for reading' box on page 37 to ensure that students understand what connectives are. You may want to write several sentences on the board using the different causal connectives listed in the box.
- To consolidate work on explanation texts, give each student a copy of **Worksheet 2.3**. They must identify which of the two examples is an explanation text, then highlight the features that make it an explanation text.

Plenary

- Invite 2 or 3 students to present their findings on **Worksheet 2.3**, using an OHT of the worksheet.

Unit 2 Tales retold

Worksheet 2.3: Which is which?

Read both texts below.
   1 Which is an explanation text? Annotate the features that make it an explanation text.
   2 What text type is the other extract?

Extract 1

> Boomerangs are probably the first heavier-than-air flying machines ever invented by human beings. The oldest Australian Aboriginal boomerangs are ten thousand years old but older hunting sticks have been discovered in Europe, where they seem to have formed part of the Stone Age arsenal of weapons.
>
> King Tutankhamun, the famous Pharaoh of ancient Egypt, who died 2,000 years ago, owned a collection of boomerangs of both the straight flying (hunting) and returning variety.
>
> No one knows for sure how the returning boomerang was first invented, but some modern boomerang-makers speculate that it developed from the flattened throwing stick, still used by the Australian Aborigines and some other tribal people around the world.

Extract 2

> A boomerang spins as it flies forward through the air. Because of this, the leading arm – the wing spinning into the direction of flight – actually travels faster than the other wing, which is spinning away from the direction of flight. This creates 'lift', which makes the boomerang turn slowly through the air.
>
> Another factor that makes a boomerang turn is the wing shape. The wings are rounded on one side and flat on the other, which causes the air to move more quickly over the top of the wing than along the bottom. Because there is greater pressure below the wing than above it, again the boomerang turns slowly and returns to the thrower's hand.

Urban legends

Tales retold

Framework Objectives

S6: Explore and compare different methods of grouping sentences into paragraphs of continuous text that are clearly focused and well developed

Wr11: Explain complex ideas and information clearly

Main text type: Explanation

Student Book pages 37–39

Starter

- Put **OHT 2.4** on the projector – a quiz testing students' knowledge of key terms that help to describe and analyse language. Students discuss in pairs which term relates to which definition and write down the correct number-letter combination. Alternatively, this can be photocopied and distributed to each pair as a worksheet.

Introduction

Focus on: Grouping sentences into paragraphs

- Read through the section with the class. Ensure that students understand how the sentence with the main point (the paragraph focus) summarises the purpose of the paragraph. Ask them how each of the paragraphs might continue, so they see how the sentences are organised in a logical way. Students may rightly point out that the two examples on page 38 also 'expand on the main point'; however, they do this in particular ways, as the annotations show.
- In question **10**, pairs analyse the paragraphs in the *How urban legends work* text in a similar way. Ask 2 or 3 pairs to present their tables to the class.

Development

Key Writing

- Read through question **11** with the class. In this question, students will write a short explanation of why urban legends are so popular. Ask pairs or small groups to brainstorm ideas. Students then choose one of these ideas and draft a paragraph on it, as if it were part of a larger explanation text on urban myths. Students can draft their paragraph working on their own or in pairs. Guide a group of students, sharing ideas and praising achievement.
- Once they have completed their draft paragraph, invite 2 or 3 students to read out their work and invite the class to comment.

Plenary

- Ask students to write down a simple explanation for why paragraphs are used, then invite 3 or 4 students to read out their explanations. Invite the class to identify clear logical steps and any causal language.

Unit 2 Tales retold

OHT 2.4: Terms and definitions

Match up the language term on the left with the correct definition on the right.

1. adjective   **A.** a word used instead of a noun or a clause to avoid repetition

2. clause   **B.** a word or phrase that links words or sentences

3. connective   **C.** a word that names an object or quality

4. noun   **D.** the most important sentence in a paragraph

5. paragraph   **E.** the form of a word that is used to refer to two or more things

6. plural   **F.** a group of words that forms the building block of a sentence

7. pronoun   **G.** a section of a piece of writing, used as an organizational tool

8. topic sentence   **H.** a word that describes something

Tales retold

Lesson 5

Framework Objective

S3: Make good use of the full range of punctuation
Main text type: Analysis

Student Book pages 40–44

Starter

- Ask students to pair up and give each pair a set of punctuation cards cut out from **Worksheet 2.5**. Their task is to match the name cards (in capitals) with the punctuation mark, then allocate one of the function cards to each. After the task, invite several pairs to feed back. To extend this task for more advanced students, ask whether there is another function for some of these punctuation marks that could also go on the card. Finally, brainstorm the overall purpose of punctuation with the class.

Introduction

- Read the article with the class and check that difficult words are understood. Ask questions about the content of the text to check basic understanding.

Key Reading

- Go through the key features of analysis texts as shown in the text-type box on page 42. Check understanding by asking students:
  – *What does 'analyse' mean?*
  – *What sorts of things count as evidence?*
  – *Name one causal connective of cause and effect, and one time connective.*
- Students discuss questions **1** to **4** in pairs. They may need a prompt with question **3**, since there is no textual link between the main text and the second quotation in the margin (which is an earlier version of the Robin Hood story). It will help if students think of the quotation as evidence to support the main point in paragraph 3. Invite 2 or 3 pairs to feed back their answers and invite the class to comment.

Development

Purpose

- For question **5**, students discuss in pairs the options as to the main purpose of the text, then feed back their decision to the class. Their choice must be supported with textual evidence.

Reading for meaning

- Students attempt questions **6** to **9** working on their own or in pairs. The focus in questions **6** and **7** is on close reading and retrieving information from the text; students should be briefed as to this requirement. Ensure that in question **8** students understand what the term 'first-person references' means, and that they need to consider the effect of using them in this analysis text.

Plenary

- Ask students to write one sentence about Robin Hood that contains two of the punctuation marks discussed in the Starter (on **Worksheet 2.5**). Invite 2 or 3 students to show what they have written and invite the class to comment on the accurate use of punctuation.

Unit 2 Tales retold

Worksheet 2.5: Punctuation functions

.	**FULL STOP**	marks the end of a sentence
,	**COMMA**	separates words or phrases in a list
?	**QUESTION MARK**	shows that the sentence is a question
!	**EXCLAMATION MARK**	shows that the sentence is shouted
'	**APOSTROPHE**	shows where a letter is missed out of a word

The growth of a legend

Tales retold

Lesson

Framework Objectives

S3: Make good use of the full range of punctuation

S&L2: Develop an idea, choosing and changing the mood, tone and pace of delivery for particular effect

Main text type: Analysis

Student Book pages 44–46

Starter

- Write the following two sentences on the board from the Robin Hood analysis text:
  - …he only used violence against the 'baddies' and only killed in self-defence.
  - …he kills Guy of Gisborne, a medieval 'bounty hunter' who is after him…
- Ask students to discuss in pairs what the quotation marks mean around the words 'baddies' and 'bounty hunter' (these terms are not to be taken literally and can be challenged).

Introduction

Focus on: The comma

- Read through the explanation of commas on pages 44–45 with the class. Make sure that students understand each of the three separate uses before they attempt question **10**, either working on their own or in pairs. Invite 2 or 3 students to feed back their answers and discuss them with the class.
- To extend this work on commas, either in class or as homework, give a copy of **Worksheet 2.6** to each student to complete.

Development

Key Speaking and Listening

- Working in pairs, students prepare a court speech as described in question **11**. Their task is to defend the good name of Robin Hood, taking any line of defence they so wish. Encourage students to back up their points by citing evidence, either from the *Analysis – Living legends* text on pages 40–41 or their own knowledge of the Robin Hood legend. Point out that drawing on evidence is one of the defining features of an analysis text. Emphasise the importance of dividing up the presentation and delivery of the speech between each pair.

Plenary

- Choose 1 or 2 pairs to deliver their speeches. The class act as a jury and decide whether Robin Hood is innocent or guilty, based on the evidence presented in each analysis. The jury should decide on the strength of the speeches (as in a debate) rather than on their own thoughts and ideas.

Unit 2 Tales retold

Worksheet 2.6: Practising the comma

1 Add commas to separate the following items or phrases in each list:

   a You will need: 450g of flour 30g of butter 500ml of milk and 1tsp of lemon juice.

   b He found the key opened the door took a ladder and climbed up onto the roof.

2 Add commas in the following sentences to show where a new clause begins:

   a Turn right at the first junction then take the second on your left.

   b Dad asked me to feed the cats although it wasn't my turn.

3 Add commas in the following sentences around the phrase that tells you more about something that has already been mentioned:

   a The floods which were the worst in living memory claimed six lives.

   b Steve Redgrave five-times Olympic champion will give a speech.

4 Tick the sentences where commas are used correctly. Put a cross against those where commas have not been used correctly.

   a The police questioned the man aged 45, who was found, running away from the scene of the crime.

   b He's a fine gymnast, an excellent runner and an even better hurdler.

   c Since you ask, I'd like to repaint the walls, change the pictures and hang new doors.

Tales retold

Lesson

Assessment Focus

AF3: Organise and present whole texts effectively, sequencing and structuring information, ideas and events

Main text type: Analysis

Student Book pages 47–49

Starter

- Write this sentence on the board: *A man goes into a pub and asks for a pint of beer and a packet of crisps*. Ask the class to write down:
  - what kind of text they think it is
  - how they know (what features in the text tell them?).
- Then ask the class what would have to be changed if this idea were to be the opening line of a novel instead of a joke. Explain that recognising these types of differences between texts will help them with the assignment.

Introduction

Stage 1

- Read through the introduction to the assignment with the class, as well as the two versions of the story and the feature boxes on page 48. Make sure that students understand the nature of the assignment, sorting out any difficulties at this early stage (for example, what 'cardboard' characters are). Ideally, give each pair a copy of **Worksheet 2.7**, which contains the full text of each urban legend. Students should then read through the stories again in pairs before discussing how the features in the boxes relate to each version.

Stage 2

- Students write notes to act as the building blocks of their report, as shown in the example on page 48 of the Student Book.

Development

Stage 3

- Each student plans their report as outlined in the Student Book.

Stage 4

- Before giving students the go ahead to draft their reports, go through the bulleted reminders on page 49. Ask for possible first sentences to introduce each paragraph and put sentence starters on the board, including some with connectives. For example: *Passage B, however, … .* Model on the board different ways of introducing evidence effectively.

Challenge

- Encourage those students who have the ability to write a short conclusion highlighting their findings and the main points of their report.

Peer Assessment

- When students have completed their reports, put them in pairs to read each others' drafts. Write up the text-type features listed below and ask students to check whether their drafts include them:
  - a clear statement of the problem in the introduction
  - good use of evidence to back up the points made
  - use of paragraphs to structure the text logically.
- Students then fill in the Peer Assessment Sheet (see page 6) and feed back their findings to the class.
- Students redraft according to suggestions.

Plenary

- Give students a copy of **OHT 2.8** (top half only) and get them to annotate the level 3 writing in groups, to show how well the student has organised the text, and what needs improvement. Then display the whole of **OHT 2.8** and ask for feedback on how to get level 3 writing up to level 4. Show in the level 4 exemplar how this can be done. Students can make changes to their own texts in light of this.

Unit 2 Tales retold

Worksheet 2.7: The Hook

Read extracts A and B and decide which is a 'story' and which is an 'urban myth'.
Discuss how each text relates to the two feature boxes on page 48 of the Student Book.

Extract A

The Hook

It was the same most evenings. Sam picked up Becky and drove his wreck to the parking area two miles outside town. There they could play the car radio full blast; they could hang out on their own.

It was already half dark when they heard the local news: '…escaped from Locksley prison…convicted for murder…'

Sam stopped drumming his fingers on the tacky steering-wheel.

'…a full-scale hunt is under way,' droned the voice on the dashboard. 'Police are advising members of the public not to approach him. He is extremely dangerous and has a hook instead of a right arm.'

'A hook!' said Becky. 'That's horrible.'

'Horrible, horrible!' said Sam, grinning in the dark.

'What was that?' cried Becky, and she jammed herself against Sam.

'What?'

'That scratching!'

'Keep your shirt on,' said Sam. 'This piece of junk's always creaking and groaning.'

'Let's go,' said Becky. 'Now, Sam. Quick!'

'If you insist,' said Sam.

'Sorry,' said Becky, when Sam pulled up outside her house. 'I just got scared. You coming in?'

Then Sam jumped up and walked round the back of the car to Becky's side. And there, hanging from the handle of Becky's door, hanging and still swinging, was a large steel hook.

Extract B

Did you hear what happened to this couple? They're friends of someone Jack knows. They're on a date, and they've driven out to a quiet country road. They hear this report on the local radio about an escaped killer with a hooked hand, and the girl's getting really nervous. He was supposed to use it on all his victims – the hook, I mean. Anyway, the girl gets so scared, and thinks she's hearing things, like a tapping on the outside of the door, and the guy's so fed up with her he revs up the car and races off. They get to her house and he drops her off, but when she gets out she turns round and there's a bloody hook hanging on the door handle.

Unit 2 Tales retold

OHT 2.8: Raising the level

Assessment Focus

AF3: Organise and present whole texts effectively, sequencing and structuring information, ideas and events

Level 3

All the features of urban legends are there.
The author addresses the reader at the start. He refers to someone who we are supposed to know.
The language is plain and like speech. Lots of they'res and they'ves are used.

Level 4

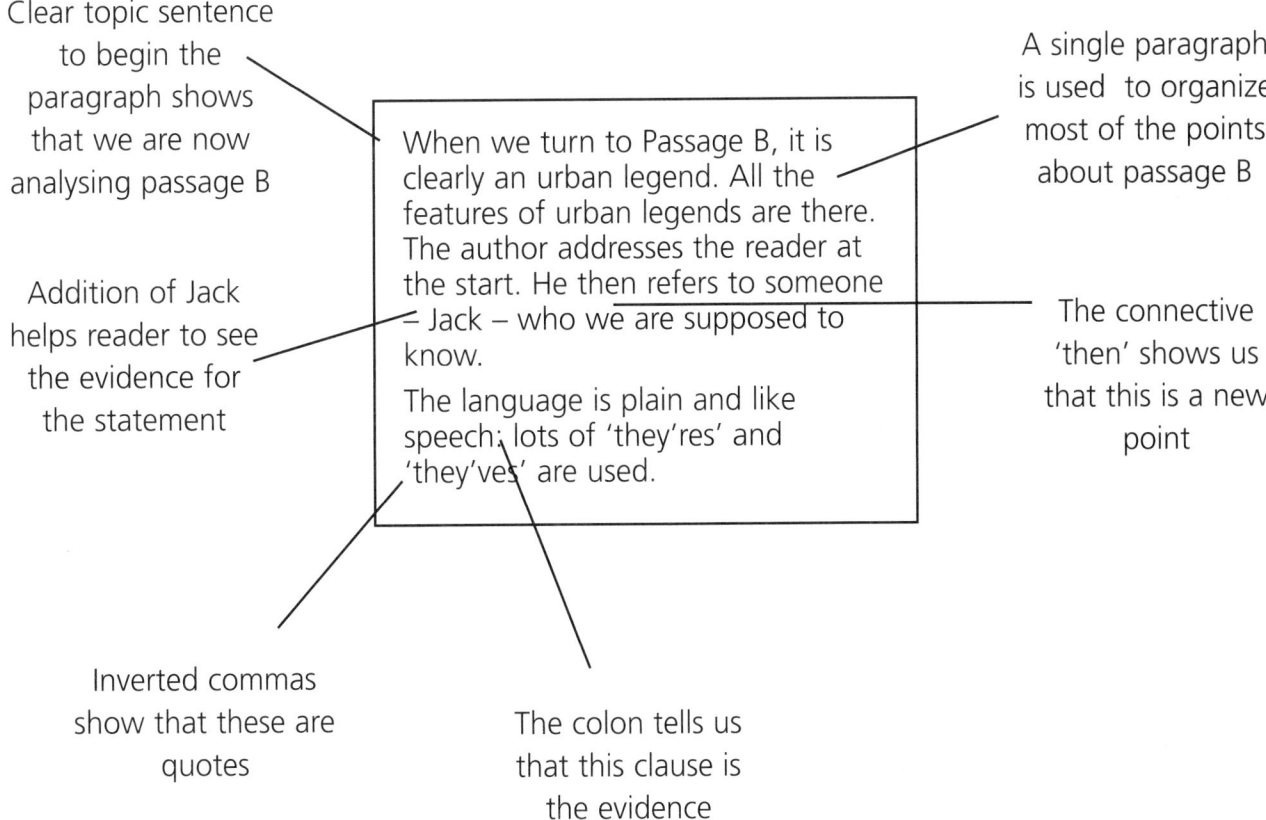

Clear topic sentence to begin the paragraph shows that we are now analysing passage B

Addition of Jack helps reader to see the evidence for the statement

When we turn to Passage B, it is clearly an urban legend. All the features of urban legends are there. The author addresses the reader at the start. He then refers to someone – Jack – who we are supposed to know.
The language is plain and like speech; lots of 'they'res' and 'they'ves' are used.

A single paragraph is used to organize most of the points about passage B

The connective 'then' shows us that this is a new point

Inverted commas show that these are quotes

The colon tells us that this clause is the evidence

Impact English Teacher's Resource © HarperCollinsPublishers 2005

Unit 3

Magic and illusion

Lesson 1

Framework Objective

R7: Identify the ways implied and explicit meanings are conveyed in different texts

Main text type: Narrative

Student Book pages 50–55

Starter

- As a check that students know how to use basic punctuation, such as capital letters, full stops, question marks and commas, write the following example on the board and ask the class to punctuate it correctly:

  the ring which Frodo held in his hand glinted he clutched it tightly would the ring exert its power over him

Introduction

- Read through the extract with the class, and check that glossary words are understood. Ask 1 or 2 students to describe what the story is about.

Key Reading

- Go through the key features of narrative texts as described in the text-type box on page 52. Explain the term 'epic', then check understanding by asking students these questions:
  - *What do you understand an epic narrative or film to mean?* (Ask students to give examples from stories or films they know.)
  - *How are the characters in epic narratives often different to those in other narratives?*
- Students complete questions **1** to **4** in pairs. If students are not familiar with *The Lord of the Rings*, they may need some prompting over the adjective 'wise' in question **2**. Ask 2 or 3 pairs to feed back their answers and invite the class to comment.

Development

Purpose

- For question **5**, pairs decide how the extract arouses the reader's curiosity about the characters and the ring. Encourage students to pinpoint evidence from the text to support their findings. Conclude by discussing how the scene anticipates Frodo's adventure, relating this back to the features of epic narratives.

Reading for meaning

- Make the distinction between literal and inferred meaning and model the examples on pages 53–54 of the Student Book. Ask students to explain how these examples show the difference between the two types of meaning, encouraging them to use terms such as 'hidden meanings' and 'reading between the lines'.
- Pairs complete questions **6a** and **b**, but before they complete the grid in **6c** they should agree on which examples have inferred meanings and what these are. Carry out a brief plenary with the class in which pairs report back with their findings.
- Next, refer students back to the work done for question **5** and introduce the term 'anticipation'. Explain that the reader anticipates what will happen next or where the story is going, as well as inferring meaning from a sentence. The same pairs can then complete **Worksheet 3.1**. Here they have to infer meaning and think of several possibilities for what might happen next.

Plenary

- Ask 2 or 3 pairs to share their findings from **Worksheet 3.1**, then discuss with the class which are the most likely. List them on the board and take a class vote on who or what the rider is (for example, is he friend or foe) and what is most likely to happen next.

Unit 3 Magic and illusion

Worksheet 3.1: The noise of hooves

In the extract from *The Lord of the Rings* below, Frodo and his friends have begun their epic adventure. They are becoming more and more aware of the many dangers ahead.

```
1   They were beginning to look out for a place off the Road, where
2   they could camp for the night, when they heard a sound that
3   brought fear back into their hearts: the noise of hooves behind
4   them. They looked back, but they could not see far because of the
5   many windings and rollings of the Road. As quickly as they could
6   they scrambled off the beaten way and up into the deep heather
7   and bilberry brushwood on the slopes above, until they came to a
8   small patch of thick-growing hazels. As they peered out from
9   among the bushes, they could see the Road, faint and grey in the
10  failing light, some thirty feet below them. The sound of hooves
11  drew nearer. They were going fast, with a light clippety-clippety-clip.
12  Then faintly, as if it was blown away from them by the breeze, they
13  seemed to catch a dim ringing, as of small bells tinkling.
```

by J.R.R. Tolkien

Discuss with your partner:

1 Which lines tell you the hobbits are afraid?

_____

2 Which lines tell you who or what the rider could be?

_____

3 What do you anticipate will happen next? (Think of more than one possibility.)
Underline the relevant parts of the text as you need to.

_____

_____

_____

Unit 3
Magic and illusion
Lesson 2

Framework Objective
W11: Appreciate the impact of figurative language in texts
Main text type: Narrative

Student Book pages 55–57

Starter

- Remind students of the basic tenses, past and present, and write the following example of the past tense on the board:
  - *Frodo, Sam and their friends began the journey after Gandalf left.*
  Ask them to change it to the present tense, then write it up:
  - *Frodo, Sam and their friends begin the journey after Gandalf leaves.*
- Point to the sense of immediacy and increased expectation when the example is written in the present tense, compared to the matter-of-fact tone when the past tense is used.

Introduction

Focus on: Reading the signs

- Introduce the term 'sign' and explain it by referring to such examples as road signs or common gestures. Ask students to think of further examples. Point out that 'symbols' often have deeper meanings, which are usually developed over time; for example, *the dove as a symbol of peace* or *the scales of justice*.
- Before students tackle question **7**, reinforce the idea of symbols by working through **OHT 3.2**. Model the examples provided and then ask the class to supply:
  - the features of the remaining symbols
  - their deeper meanings.
  Emphasise the connection between the two. For example, students may readily see that a flame (which is cross-cultural) has the features of light and fire, linking it to the symbolic meaning of 'life' or 'eternal life'. However, they may be unaware that the dove and the olive branch have a biblical meaning. Take students through each example on **OHT 3.2** before beginning to discuss the significance of the ring in the extract.
- Next, ask pairs to complete question **7**. They will need to identify the information in the extract and discuss what might be inferred together. They then complete the right-hand column of the table before deciding what the ring mainly symbolises. Invite 2 or 3 pairs to feed back to the class with their findings and conclusion.

Development

Key Writing

- Before students complete question **8**, take them through the first symbol listed (the key) and apply the bulleted questions:
  - *What is it made of?*
  - *What can it do?*
  - *What are its weaknesses?*
  - *What are its strengths?*
  For example, in answer to 'What can it do?', encourage students to come up with a range of verbs, such as *lock, unlock, close, open, hide, conceal, reveal*. In this way, students will extend the possibility of hidden meanings.
- Students should complete the work on their symbol alone, then share their ideas with a partner. Between them, each pair should choose one of their symbols.

Plenary

- Invite 2 or 3 pairs to report back on their symbol, describing one or two of its features to provide clues. The class should guess the hidden meanings of each symbol.

Unit 3 — Magic and illusion

OHT 3.2: Symbols

The following table lists seven different symbols. Complete the table to show the features and meaning of each symbol. Some examples have already been given, to start you off.

Symbol	Features	Meaning
The five rings of the Olympic flag	Rings are linked together.	Each ring stands for a quality that should be shown by Olympians. These qualities are all linked.
The Scales of Justice	Weighing scales in balanced position.	
The Tree of Life		
A heart		
A dove	White bird with leafy branch.	
Old Father Time		
A flame		

Impact English Teacher's Resource © HarperCollinsPublishers 2005

Unit 3
Magic and illusion
Lesson 3

Framework Objective

R10: Analyse the overall structure of a text to identify how key ideas are developed (through the organisation of the content)
Main text type: Poetry

Student Book pages 58–62

Starter

- Write 'rhythm' and 'rhyme' on the board. Ask students to distinguish between the two, since they are often confused. Explain that a regular rhythm will almost certainly rhyme (as in the poem in Unit 1, pages 11–12), and that the rhyme helps to move the rhythm along. Introduce the idea that free verse may contain hidden rhymes.

Introduction

- Read through the poem, explaining how the poet has based his work on an idea from a story by Nikolai Gogol. Ask 1 or 2 students to explain what the poem is about.

Key Reading

- Go through the key features of poetry as shown in the text-type box on page 60. Check understanding by asking students:
  – What is the difference between rhythm and rhyme?
  This should be easier, given the work done in the Starter.
- Ask students to describe a strong rhythm. They can do this with reference to music, such as a favourite pop song. Remind them of the difference between a regular and an irregular rhythm in poetry. To demonstrate how a free verse poem has rhythm, read a short piece of prose to the class and ask students to listen carefully for the pauses, particularly at the end of sentences. Then read part of the poem again. Ask students to compare the two, describing the differences. Elicit that the voice rises and falls far more as it follows the lines of the poem than it does with prose.
- Students complete questions **1** to **4** in pairs. Note in particular their answers to questions **3** and **4**, in light of the preliminary discussion.

Development

Purpose

- Arguably any of the choices in question **5** might fit, but students should discuss them fully. Pairs round off this section by feeding back with their ideas. Make sure that they point to examples in the poem as evidence.

Reading for meaning

- Explain how *The Nose* is a simple fantasy that shares features of a folk tale. Run through the features of folk tales in question **6a**, pointing out that folk tales are found in all cultures and belong to an oral tradition. Then ask students to complete **Worksheet 3.3** in small groups. Help them to select a tale from a range of cultures. Not all folk tales will have the same features as those listed (although most will have several). Students should record any additional features they note. They will then be better prepared to complete the rest of question **6**.

Plenary

- Ask groups to report back on their findings from **Worksheet 3.3**. Draw up the heading 'Character traits' on the board. Students should consider the traits of the main characters in their folk tales:
  – *What did they do when faced with danger?*
  – *Were they resourceful?*
  – *Did they escape or were they rescued?*
- Discuss the similarities and the differences between the poem *The Nose* and the folk tale, highlighting the main differences between the nose itself and the folk tale hero or heroine.

Unit 3 — Magic and illusion

Worksheet 3.3: Folk tale features

Think of a folk or fairy tale you know (such as *Hansel and Gretel* or *Ali Baba and the Forty Thieves*). Map out its simple structure using the table below.

Title of folk tale	
Introduction (opening)	
Complication (problem arises)	
Crisis (a big moment or event)	
Resolution (ending)	

Tick the following features which your fairy or folk tale also has.

Features of the folk tale:	The main character:
strange characters or creatures	seeks adventure
strange events	meets danger
a journey	may escape by magic
	outwits enemy
	may be freed from a spell
	triumphs in the end

What other features does your folk or fairy tale have?

_____

_____

_____

Magic and illusion

Framework Objective

Wr7: Experiment with different language choices to imply meaning and to establish the tone of a piece

Main text type: Poetry

Student Book pages 62–64

Thesauruses should be made available.

Starter

- Explain the difference between a simile and a metaphor. Then write on the board:
  - *A simile compares one thing with another using 'like' or 'as'. For example, 'As slow as a snail.'*
  - *A metaphor describes one thing as <u>being</u> another. For example, 'The milky face in the sky.'*
- Brainstorm more examples of both similes and metaphors with the class. Stress that students' choice of words should suit the objects compared.

Introduction

Focus on: Building images

- Remind students what an image is by referring back to the text-type box on page 60 of the Student Book. Point out that using similes and metaphors is a way of building images. Explain that images often appeal to the senses.
- Students complete question **7** by identifying the images in *The Nose* that appeal to the sense of smell; for example, 'sniffing at everything' (line 5) and 'the world was so full of scents' (line 12).
- Revisit the difference between similes and metaphors through the 'Grammar for reading' box on page 62, then ask students to complete question **8** working on their own. Students can work in pairs to complete the spidergram in question **9a** (for which thesauruses should be made available). However, they should create their own similes and metaphors for questions **9b** and **10b**.

Development

Key Writing

- Students write a free verse poem about the mouth that gobbles up the nose for question **11**. Once students have worked out their story plan in question **11a** they can begin to write their poems. Advise them to keep the story simple, to fit the purpose of their poem.
- Those students that find it difficult to write in lines successfully may find **Worksheet 3.4** useful in providing them with some direction. Remind students that they can adapt the writing frame, adding lines and ideas or dropping prompts as necessary. Students should try to include similes and metaphors, drawing on their work for questions **9** and **10**, and remember to give their poem a title.

Plenary

- Ask students to give examples of the similes and metaphors used in their poems. Then turn to their story structures. Note common features on the board and how far students have used *The Nose* as a model or given the 'mouth' the same outcome. Ask them to consider the senses 'sight' and 'sound' and how 'eyes' and 'ears' might fare in the same circumstances.
- Referring back to the hero/heroine of the folk tale, students should conclude by considering which, of all the senses, would have the best chance of survival. (Would it be the 'eyes' since they could see danger coming?)

Unit 3 — Magic and illusion

Worksheet 3.4: Poetry frame

Use this frame to help you write your free verse poem about the mouth. Add to the lines or change any to suit your ideas.

Once

there was a mouth,

A mouth with _____

A mouth that _____

It was a mouth that wanted _____

And so _____

At first all was well, all was _____

Everything was _____

The mouth felt like _____

It was _____

Until it met with _____

And because it met with _____

Everything _____

The mouth was _____

It was _____

It was _____

And so _____

Magic and illusion

Lesson 5

Framework Objectives

R3: Make notes in different ways, choosing a form which suits the purpose

Wr11: Explain complex ideas and information clearly

Main text type: Explanation

Student Book pages 65–69

Starter

- Remind students that phrases can expand sentences and add interest or detail. Write the following sentences that contain prepositional phrases on the board (the first is from the Derren Brown text):
  - *The wall outside my house is not 4ft high.*
  - *Leon is cooking in the kitchen.*
  - *Millie is at the station, with her bag.*
- Explain the term 'preposition' and ask students to identify the prepositional phrases. Encourage them to add another phrase, ensuring that the meaning is clear.

Introduction

- Read through the website text with the class. Ask 1 or 2 students what the explanation is about.

Key Reading

- Go through the key features of explanation texts as described in the text-type box on page 67. Check understanding by asking students:
  - *Think of examples of a common process that might need explanation.* (For example, the life cycle of the butterfly: eggs are laid; larva hatches; larva outgrows skin; turns into pupa; butterfly emerges.)
  - *How would you need to organise this explanation?* (For example, in logical steps, perhaps using subheadings or diagrams.)
- Students complete questions **1**, **2** and **3** in pairs. Focus on those features of the text which were not covered in the example above, in particular causal language.

Development

Purpose

- For question **4**, guide students towards the correct option by asking them what kind of text it is (i.e. so they choose the '*why* the tricks work' option).

Reading for meaning

- From the outset it is important that students distinguish between description and explanation in the text. Run through paragraph 1 with the class, pointing out that:
  - sentence 1 is part commentary and part explanation
  - the middle section describes the sentence
  - the last sentence of the paragraph is explanation.
  Relate this to the example in the Student Book on page 68, showing students how the connectives 'so' and 'because' link cause and effect.
- Ask students to complete **Worksheet 3.5** in groups and report back. Carry out a short plenary to find out whether they have understood the difference between 'so' and 'because' and are able to apply other suitable connectives.
- The same groups should now be able to work confidently and systematically through questions **5** and **6**. Remind students to keep their notes for use in question **8**.

Plenary

- Write the headings 'Description' and 'Explanation' on the board. Ask groups to report back from their notes, identifying the correct information for each type of text. Conclude by recapping the main features of explanation texts.

Impact English Teacher's Resource © HarperCollinsPublishers 2005

Unit 3 Magic and illusion

Worksheet 3.5: Making connections

1 Join up these sentences, using the connectives '**so**' or '**because**'.

a Derren Brown plays tricks. He wants to find out people's reactions.
_____
_____

b The wallet was filled with cash. Derren Brown wanted to see if people would pick it up.
_____
_____

c The wallet looked suspicious. No one picked it up.
_____
_____

d A line was drawn around the wallet. Everyone walked past.
_____
_____

e Most people ignore a ringing phone in a public phone box. They know it has nothing to do with them.
_____
_____

f Derren Brown wants to confuse people. He bombards them with instructions.
_____
_____

g People fall asleep in phone boxes. Derren Brown has played a trick on them.
_____
_____

2 Replace 'so' or 'because' with one of the following connectives:

therefore   *since*

consequently   *as a result.*

Write the connectives you choose next to the sentences. Each sentence should keep the same meaning.

Trick of the mind

Magic and illusion

Framework Objective

S2: Explore the impact of a variety of sentence structures
Main text type: Explanation

Student Book pages 69–70

Starter

- Point out that a phrase needs to be positioned appropriately in a sentence, otherwise the original meaning of the sentence may be altered. Write the following sentences on the board:
  - *They saw the hot-air balloon on the way to the beach.*
  - *The wasp stung the man in a sudden fit of temper.*
  - *He presented the football cup with a beaming grin.*
- Ask pairs to identify the ambiguity in each sentence and reposition the phrase.

Introduction

Focus on: The active and the passive

- Introduce the terms 'active' and 'passive' and explain the difference between them. Point out how the former is lively and direct, hence 'active', while the latter is used in more formal situations, for example, when explaining the reason why something happens.
- Take students through the first example (on page 69 of the Student Book) carefully, ensuring they understand the terms 'subject', 'verb' and 'object'. Check understanding by asking students to offer further examples.
- Next, compare this example with the one on page 70. Ensure that students have grasped:
  - how the object has changed places in the sentence, becoming the subject
  - the change in the verb
  - the introduction of the agent for the 'by phrase'.
- Students complete the transformations in question **7** on their own before comparing their answers with a partner's.

Development

Key Writing

- Before students begin question **8**, quickly refer them to **OHT 3.6**. This short annotated extract illustrates nicely how a description precedes an explanation.
- Encourage students to organise their own writing in a similar fashion and write this short prompt on the board: *Description first, explanation second*. Stress, however, that they should begin their explanation with a new paragraph; students could also include a subheading. Add these points to the advice on the board, along with the bullet points in the book. Since students will be recalling the information from memory, this organisational advice is vital.

Plenary

- Ask students to describe what the active is and the kind of writing it produces. Similarly, ask them to give a definition of the passive. Record their comments and discuss with the class, correcting any errors.
- Recap the main features of explanation texts, then select 2 or 3 students to read aloud their explanation of the abandoned wallet trick. Invite the class to comment on those features that worked well and also any others that might have been included. List any features omitted on the board.

Unit 3 — Magic and illusion

OHT 3.6: The lost taxi driver

This is another of Derren Brown's tricks. Note how he has organised it.

Begins with a description of the events. Gives considerable detail, so the reader has a clear picture of what is happening

> When I get in a taxi, I immediately bombard the driver with a story about a wheel of a toy car that I've lost and how I've had a really silly day going around and round in circles looking for it. He is trying to think of how to get to the London Eye but I keep distracting him by talking about unrelated things. My talking becomes an anchor in his thought processes, always bringing him back to his inability to find the London Eye.

Starts explanation. Begins to give clues about why the taxi driver is lost

The main part of the explanation. The 'anchor' blocks the driver's memory of the route to the London Eye

Unit 3 Assignment

Magic and illusion

Lesson

Assessment Focus

AF5: Vary sentences for clarity, purpose and effect
Main text type: Explanation

Student Book pages 71–73

Starter

- Brainstorm some common connectives with the class, asking students to describe their function (for example, 'because' is cause and effect, 'now' is temporal). Also point out that the relative pronouns 'who' and 'which' can connect sentences. Ask students to change the following sentences into Standard English using the correct pronoun:
  - *He's the magician what pulls the ten-pound note out of the hat.*
  - *There's the ten-pound note, what came out of the magician's hat.*

Introduction

Stage 1

- Remind students of the difference between description and explanation, then read the description of the trick with the class. Ask students to describe the scenario in which this trick would take place (for example, a stage on which they, as the magician, would perform the trick). Students should also identify which tense the passage is written in (the present tense). Point to the first sentence, asking students to note how it describes a sequence of events. For example, they could say: *First, ask six members of the audience…* Students should supply other time or sequence connectives, such as 'secondly' and 'then'.

Development

Stage 2

- Draw students' attention to the notes as explanation and not description. Pairs read through the notes to grasp how the trick works, then clarify points through discussion. When reporting back, check that all students understand how the trick works.

Stage 3

- Students begin a full draft, using their notes and referring to the bullet point advice in the Student Book (page 73). Remind them to vary their sentences by using suitable connectives and the relative pronouns 'who' and 'which'.
- Encourage students with the time and ability to use connectives that help to sequence events. This will greatly aid the logic of their writing. They may also like to experiment with the passive tense.
- To extend this work, students can complete **Worksheet 3.7**, which offers practice in selecting appropriate connectives and correcting errors in a series of sentences.

Peer Assessment

- When students have finished their writing, they work in pairs and assess each other's drafts. Write up the following text-type features on the board:
  - present tense
  - first person singular and plural (I / we)
  - using causal connectives.
  Students check whether these features have been included in their drafts.
- They then fill in the Peer Assessment Sheet (see page 6) and feed back their findings.
- Students redraft according to suggestions.

Plenary

- Give a copy of **OHT 3.8** (top half only) to groups and get students to annotate the level 3 writing to show how well the student has varied their sentences, and what needs improvement. Then display the whole of **OHT 3.8** and ask for feedback on how to get the level 3 writing up to level 4. Show in the exemplar of level 4 how this can be done. Students can make changes to their own texts in light of this.

Unit 3 Magic and illusion

Worksheet 3.7: A tricky business

Read the sentences below.
- Some need a connective.
- Some have mistakes in them – these are shown in **bold**.
- Some are two sentences that could be turned into one by using a connective.

Correct or improve each sentence by writing it out again underneath.

1 I must have an accomplice **what** is reliable.

_____

2 …I begin the trick, I prepare myself and keep calm.

_____

3 Most people are fooled by the trick **where** they see it.

_____

4 We must be sure not to give anything away. That will ruin the trick.

_____

5 People in the audience want to be entertained. I must perform well.

_____

6 If I make a mistake I don't worry **so** I can usually cover it up.

_____

7 …I perform the trick badly I get annoyed with myself.

_____

Unit 3: Magic and illusion

OHT 3.8: Raising the level

Assessment Focus
AF5: Vary sentences for clarity, purpose and effect

Level 3

Next, I collect up all the envelopes. I place my accomplice's envelope at the bottom of the pile. Then I pick up the top envelope. I look into it with my x-ray eyes. I spell out the word cabbage. My accomplice says the word cabbage and looks amazed. I open the envelope and read the false word cabbage. To myself I read the real word written down.

Level 4

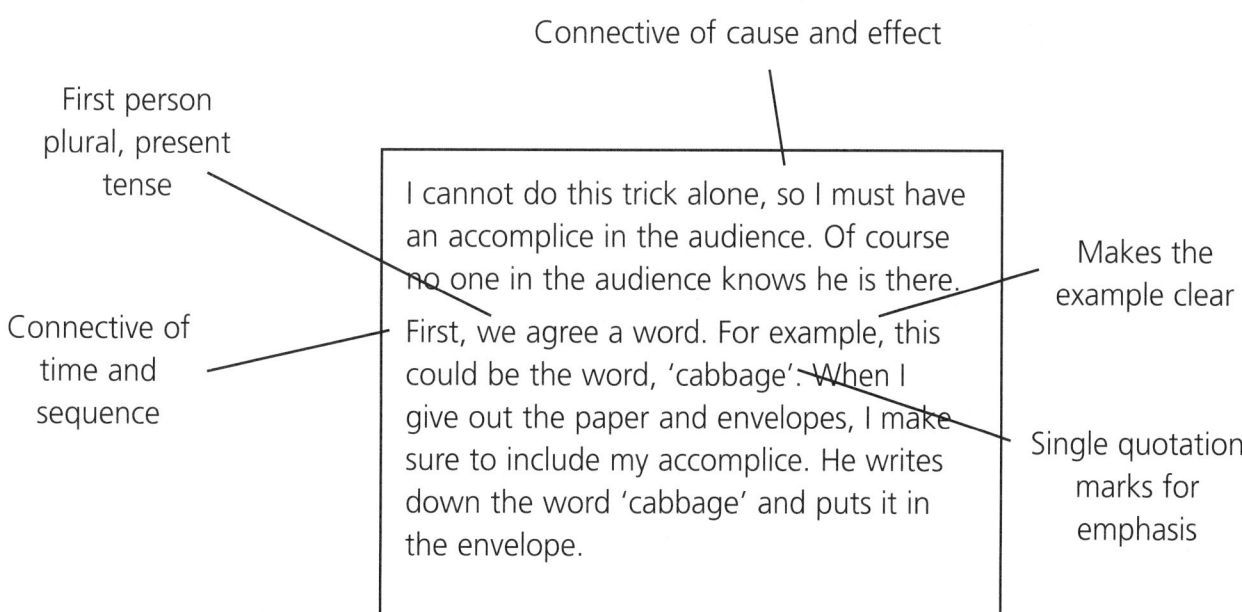

Connective of cause and effect

First person plural, present tense

Connective of time and sequence

I cannot do this trick alone, so I must have an accomplice in the audience. Of course no one in the audience knows he is there. First, we agree a word. For example, this could be the word, 'cabbage'. When I give out the paper and envelopes, I make sure to include my accomplice. He writes down the word 'cabbage' and puts it in the envelope.

Makes the example clear

Single quotation marks for emphasis

Unit 4
Destructive nature
Lesson 1

Framework Objective
W1b: Review, consolidate and secure spelling conventions (pluralisation)
Main text type: Information

Student Book pages 74–78

Starter

- Point out the word 'tornado' in the text and its plural 'tornadoes'. Reinforce the plural rule of adding '–es' to words that end in 'o' by offering the following pairs:
  - *volcano / volcanoes*
  - *potato / potatoes*
  - *tomato / tomatoes*
  - *hero / heroes*
  - *echo / echoes*
- Note some exceptions to this rule (for example, *radios* and *pianos*.) Then mention the verb 'does', which students often spell as 'dose'. It may be useful for them to recall the plural noun for female deer ('does') and its meaning, since the two words, though spelled the same, are pronounced differently. Explain that they are homographs.

Introduction

- Read through the information text with the class, and check that glossary words are understood. Ask 1 or 2 students to explain what the story is about.

Key Reading

- Go through the key features of information texts as described in the text-type box on page 76. Check understanding by asking students these questions:
  - *What visual elements might an information text include?*
  - *What do we call examples that support the points we make?*
  - *What are the differences between explanation, instruction and information texts?*
- Pairs should offer examples of hybrid texts (for example, an information text on cars that also explains how an engine works and gives instructions on how to change a tyre).
- Students then complete questions **1** to **4** in pairs, which cover the other features of information texts and feed back to the class.

Development

Purpose

- Students should be able to recognise that the text is mainly an information text but also includes an explanation of how tornadoes form, which is hidden in the first paragraph. In question **5**, point them towards the causal language that indicates where the explanation begins in paragraph 1 ('This clash leads to…').

Reading for meaning

- Before students complete question **6**, refer them back to question **4** and point out that:
  - illustrations provide information (in addition to that in the text)
  - subheadings are easy to access and guide the reader to particular information.
- Discuss how the information under 'The Alley' could be made more accessible for readers (for example, *as facts presented in a diagram, annotations on a map, or as a chart*). Students then complete the chart in question **7b**, working in pairs if preferred.
- For question **8**, students turn to paragraph 2 of the extract and find the advice given. **Worksheet 4.1** can be used to extend this activity.

Plenary

- Draw a three-column chart on the board. Head the first column 'Information' and ask students to recall as many features of information texts as they can. Then ask them to name the other text types covered (explanations and instructions) and identify features of these evident in the extract. For example:
  - Explanation: third person, present tense, technical vocabulary.
  - Instruction: imperative verbs, present tense, step-by-step points, simple vocabulary.

Unit 4 — Destructive nature

Worksheet 4.1: Tornadoes

1 Read the following paragraph from *Tornado Alley*.

> ### Twister!
>
> It is no good trying to simply outrun a tornado – it will almost certainly catch up with you. Anyone outside when a tornado approaches should try and move quickly away from the storm's path. If there is no time to escape the tornado's path, it is best to lie flat in the nearest ditch. Some houses in high-risk areas have an underground storm cellar for protection.

2 Underline those words in the text that give advice about what to do if a tornado approaches. Look for verbs that can become imperative.

3 Now you are going to rewrite the advice to make it sound more urgent. You will need to change the layout, language and punctuation.

The rewriting has been started for you below. Note the changes and then complete the advice by adding more bullet points, using the imperative.

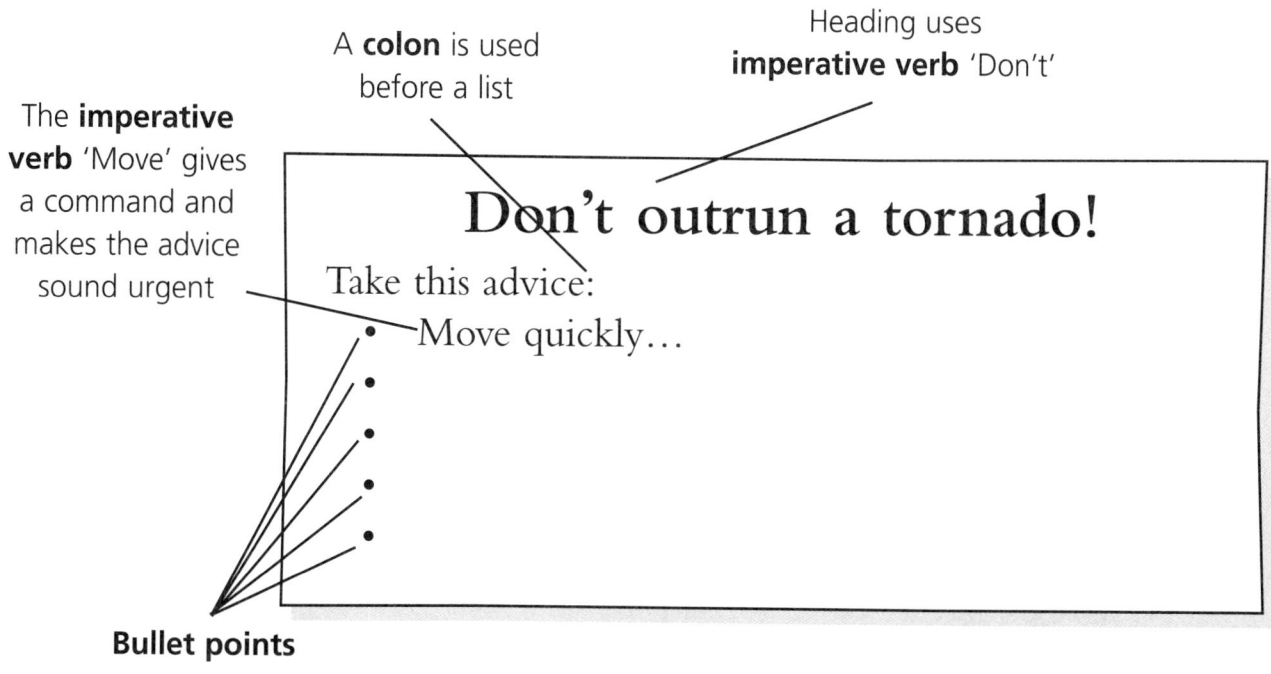

4 What extra advice would you add? For example, what advice would you give if you were indoors but had no storm cellar? Add this advice to the list.

Unit 4
Destructive nature
Lesson 2

Framework Objectives

W1b: Review, consolidate and secure spelling conventions (pluralisation)

R2: Undertake independent research using a range of reading strategies, applying their knowledge of how texts and ICT databases are organised and acknowledging sources

Wr10: Organise and present information, selecting and synthesising appropriate material and guiding the reader clearly through the text

Main text type: Information

Student Book pages 78–79

Starter

- Remind students of the plural spelling rule:
  - For words ending in 'y' preceded by a vowel, add '–s'. For example, *key/keys*, *quay/quays*, *donkey/donkeys*, *monkey/monkeys*.
  - For words ending in 'y' preceded by a consonant, drop the 'y' and add '–ies'. For example, *lorry/lorries*, *cherry/cherries*, *supply/supplies*, *daisy/daisies*, and the frequently confused *dairy/dairies* and *diary/diaries*.
- Ask students to spell a selection of these words.

Introduction

Focus on: Carrying out research

- This section asks students to carry out research into tornadoes. Students should be experienced in dealing with databases but they may still experience difficulties in locating and selecting useful information on websites. If they have access to a multimedia centre or a well-equipped library, they may find useful information on CD-Roms for question **9**. If students are carrying out their research on the Internet, reinforce the need to choose the best key words and ask the right questions. Refer them to the advice on using search engines on page 78.
- Before students begin their research, hand out **Worksheet 4.2** to pairs and go through the research process with them. The worksheet should help them to focus on the topic at hand and select appropriate information. Once they have found relevant information they will need to create their own document and save it, so they can refer to it in question **10**. Students should also record their sources in this file.

Development

Key Writing

- Run through question **10**, making sure that students understand they are writing an opening statement and producing a table of information, following the instructions given on page 79. They should give some thought to how they will organise and present their texts and tables so that the information is easy to access. As well as considering a title for their texts, they should come up with subheadings. Ask whether they will keep the subheadings they created in their files for question **9** or change them. Students should print off their finished work for presentation in the Plenary.

Plenary

- Divide the class into small groups. Each group should read each others' work and discuss how they carried out the research, focusing on the following:
  - *What was the most useful information found?*
  - *Was there any information that was difficult to find?*
  - *Did you experience any particular difficulties using ICT?*
- Each group should recap the main points of their discussion, then appoint a member to report back to the class. Afterwards, summarise the best information and highlight the main points that emerge on each of the research methods. Students may like to display their finished work.

Unit 4 Destructive nature

Worksheet 4.2: Tornadoes in Texas

Use this flowchart to help you when you are searching for data about tornadoes.

Remember: you should not use the Internet without your teacher's guidance.

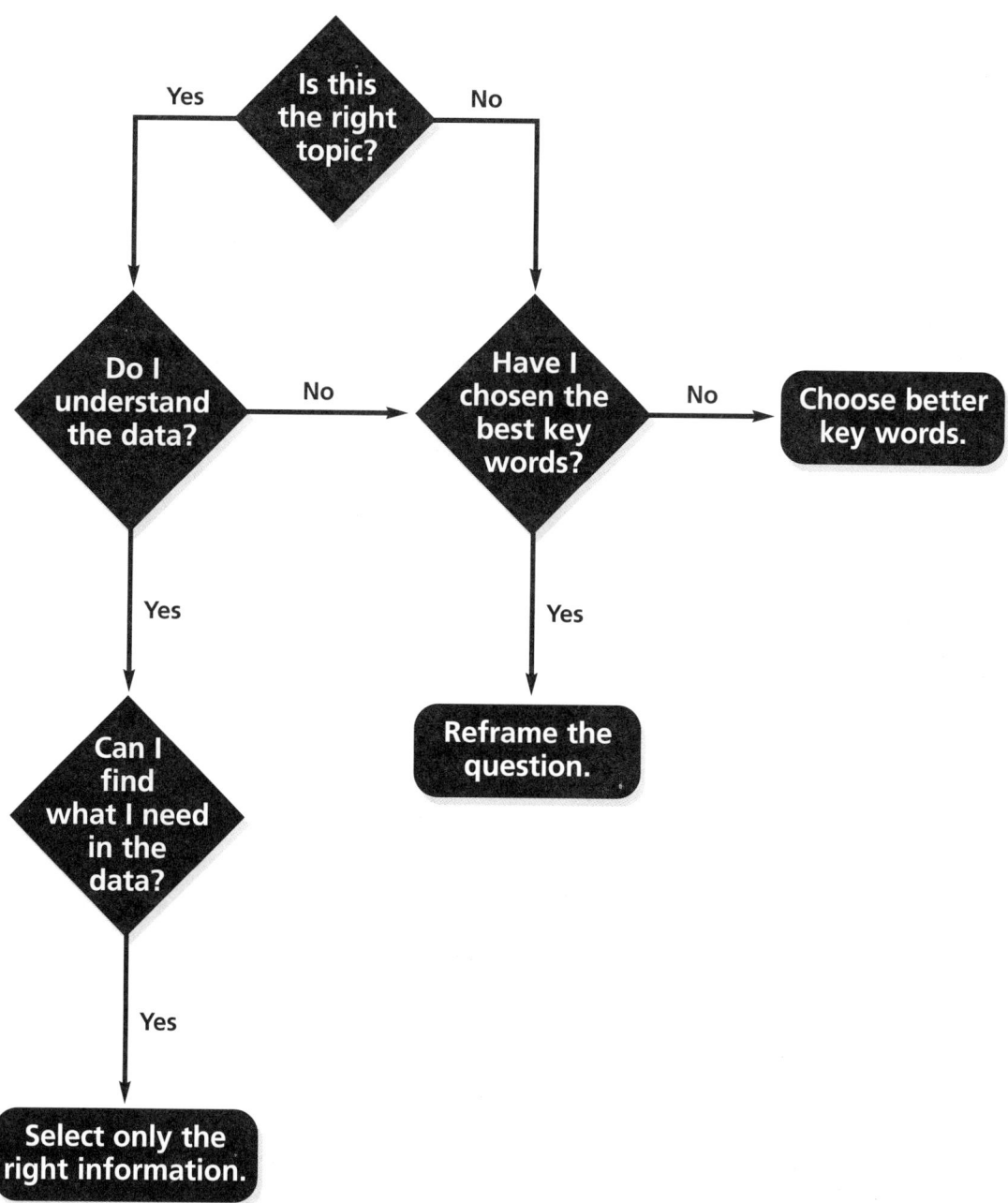

Bee attack

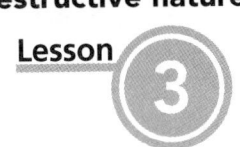
Destructive nature

Lesson 3

Framework Objectives

W1f: Review, consolidate and secure spelling conventions (homophones)

S6: Explore and compare different methods of grouping sentences into paragraphs of continuous text that are clearly focused and well developed (by chronology)

Main text type: Recount

Student Book pages 80–84

Starter

- Check students can spell the following common homophones:
  - weather / whether
  - there / their / they're
  - which / witch
  - allowed / aloud
  - you're / your
  - would / wood
  - knew / new
  - to / too / two.
- Point out that since homophones are more commonly misspelled in continuous prose, students should check their work regularly, even though they may know the spellings.

Introduction

- Read through the recount together, checking that glossary words are understood. Ask 1 or 2 students to describe what the story is about.

Key Reading

- Go through the key features of recount texts as described in the text-type box on page 82. Check understanding by asking students:
  - Define the term 'autobiography'.
  - Explain why an autobiography is a recount, giving examples of autobiographies you know.
- Ask pairs to complete questions **1**, **2** and **3**, drawing attention to the time span referred to in the text (six months) and contrasting this with the probable time span of the main event (the attack). Ask pairs to feed back and invite the class to comment.

Development

Purpose

- Pairs choose the main purpose of the recount from the options provided in question **4**. It may help if they think why they would write about such an event if it happened to them. Encourage students to refer to evidence from the text.

Reading for meaning

- Help students to isolate the main points in paragraph 1 of the recount. They can then work in pairs to complete their timelines for the remaining paragraphs, following the example given on page 83. Once they have completed questions **5** and **6**, ask 2 or 3 students to report back to ensure the timelines are generally accurate.
- Give **Worksheet 4.3** to students and discuss the example of added detail, which is based on the extract. Point out that by using connectives students can add detail that extends the meaning as well as the appeal of their sentences. Students list their own connectives at first; the whole class could then share ideas to produce a fuller list. By drawing on sentences from the timeline, students will also create a chronology in their writing; this will be useful to refer to later in the 'Key Writing' task (question **8**).

Plenary

- Invite 3 or 4 students to read out their sentences from **Worksheet 4.3**. Write interesting examples on the board in random order. Discuss the events surrounding each sentence, then invite the class to help you sort the events chronologically.

Unit 4 Destructive nature

Worksheet 4.3: Adding detail

Compare these two sentences:

> His pony threw him to the dust.

The time connective 'when' adds detail in time order

> His pony threw him to the dust when the bees viciously attacked.

You could also write this sentence the other way around:

> When the bees viciously attacked, his pony threw him into the dust.

Note how a comma is added

1 Write different kinds of connectives under these headings. Some examples have already been given.

Time/Sequence	Adding	Comparing
until, meanwhile	as well as	in the same way

2 a Choose four sentences from your timeline for *Buzzing Death*. Choose two sentences from during the attack and two sentences from after the attack.

b Use some of your connectives from question 1 to add detail to the sentences.

3 Vary your writing style by adding detail before as well as after your sentences.

Keep your work to refer to later for the Key Writing task (question 8).

Destructive nature

Framework Objectives

- **W1c:** Review, consolidate and secure spelling conventions (word endings)
- **W11:** Appreciate the impact of figurative language in texts
- **R3:** Make notes in different ways, choosing a form which suits the purpose
- **Main text type:** Recount

Student Book pages 84–85

 Thesauruses should be available.

Starter

- Write some common, regular verbs on the board with their simple past tense or present participle endings. For example, 'hope' + '–ing'; 'try' + '–ed'; 'hum' + '–ing'. Ask students to swap the endings round on the stem verbs, spelling each new word correctly. Note any common errors and remind students of the rules.

Introduction

Focus on: Creating images

- Draw students' attention to the way in which the writer of *Buzzing Death* uses powerful verbs to create images and the effect this has on the reader. Students then complete question **7**, using a thesaurus to collect as many synonyms for the verbs on page 85 as they can. Discuss how some of these verbs might be used in a sentence. For example, students could begin a sentence with a non-finite verb:
  – *Crunching* them with my teeth I spat the bees out in panic.
  Or they could use more than one main verb:
  – I *shrieked, sobbed, howled*, but no one came.

- To extend this work, hand out **Worksheet 4.4**, explaining that the verbs highlighted in the paragraph need replacing with more vivid verbs. Ask pairs to draw on the stock of verbs they collected for question **7** and any other suitable verbs they can think of. Students should record all new verbs that they use. Alternatively, you may prefer to work through this activity with the whole class, using an OHT version of **Worksheet 4.4** and discussing why some suggestions are more successful than others.

Development

Key Writing

- Students work in pairs to complete the table in question **8a**, sharing ideas and using *Buzzing Death* as a model. Once they have a rough plan, they complete question **8b**, drafting their paragraphs on their own. Encourage students to draw on work previously done to produce a successful recount, including the verbs they collected for question **7** and **Worksheets 4.3** and **4.4**. Remind students that they should write in the first person and the past tense, as if writing an autobiography. Those who have difficulty getting started could use the example on page 85 of the Student Book; otherwise students should try to think of their own opening sentences.

Plenary

- Ask a range of students to give a brief summary of their recount, describing the main events under each section ('Before', 'During' and 'After' the attack). Invite several students to read their descriptions aloud. Highlight powerful verbs and any other well-chosen verbs, showing how they help to develop sentences. Finally, recap the main features of an autobiography, asking students to identify these in their written work.

Unit 4 Destructive nature

Worksheet 4.4: Powerful verbs

The following paragraph contains some common verbs. Find the verbs and replace them with more exciting verb choices. You could use the bank of verbs you have already collected (for question 7 in your textbook) for ideas.

> Everyone looked up, pointing into the distance. The sky was dense, crammed full with insects. Before I knew it the cloud was coming towards me. Suddenly there were insects everywhere. I brushed them off my clothes. I pulled them from my hair. I picked them off my skin. Waving my arms in the air, I began to call out. I began to run, shouting at the top of my voice, but no one heard.

Unit 4

The Birds

Destructive nature

Lesson 5

Framework Objective

S3: Make good use of the full range of punctuation
Main text type: Narrative

Student Book pages 86–91

Starter

- Ask students whether they know:
  - how and when to use speech marks
  - where other punctuation, such as commas, full stops or question marks occurs in direct speech.
- Write the following sentence on the board and ask students to punctuate it accurately:
  I don't know what it all means she said are we in danger from the birds

Introduction

- Read through the text with the class, checking that glossary words are understood. Ask 1 or 2 students to describe what this episode is about.

Key Reading

- Go through the key features of narrative texts as described in the text-type box on page 88. Check understanding by asking students:
  - *Think of several features of non-fiction texts that contrast with these narrative features* (the use of formal and technical language, the use of the passive tense).
  - *Where is formal technical language used in the extract?*
- Students complete questions **1** and **2** in pairs. To help them with question **3**, refer students back to the discussion in **Lesson 1** on contrasting text types. (The change in style is discussed more fully again in **Lesson 6**.) Pairs then feed back to the class.

Development

Purpose

- Introduce this section by highlighting how the writer sparks our interest in the opening sentence – the reader immediately knows that something is wrong. Discuss questions **4** and **5** with students. They should deduce that the attack by the birds is not mentioned until the end of the paragraph, to create suspense.

Reading for meaning

- Read through the example sentence (on page 89 of the Student Book) and discuss the effects of using long sentences in prose. Point to the way in which the long sentence helps to make the writing flow and accentuates the vivid imagery. Also discuss how the pace is maintained, drawing a contrast with the example on page 90. Students should then complete question **6**, to create a flowing sentence of their own. Note any punctuation errors.
- Work through the text on extending sentences on page 90 of the Student Book, noting the variety created when sentences begin with '–ing' verbs (avoid mentioning the term 'non-finite verbs'). As students begin question **7**, hand out **Worksheet 4.5**. Guide the class through the planning frame, helping students to make their choices. For example, discuss how the use of the present tense will make their writing seem more immediate. Praise students' best choices. The whole class should develop a clear picture of the setting and creature they are writing about before they begin writing their paragraphs.

Plenary

- Students should work in small groups of no more than 3. Ask each group to select example sentences from their descriptions that use non-finite verbs. Students could also identify any extended sentences. Each group should then share their choices with the class.

Impact English Teacher's Resource © HarperCollinsPublishers 2005

Unit 4 Destructive nature

Worksheet 4.5: Trapped

Use this planning frame to help you write a vivid paragraph about a trapped creature.

Creature
- What kind?
- What is it like?
- Is it large, small, young, old?

_____
_____
_____
_____

Setting
- Whose room is it?
- Does it have any important features?

_____
_____
_____
_____

Tense/Person
(tick which one)
- Past tense ☐
- Present tense ☐
- First person (I/we) ☐
- Third person (he/she/it) ☐

_____
_____
_____

Useful verbs
- ending in '–ed'
- ending in '–ing'

_____
_____
_____
_____

Other useful vocabulary
(nouns, adjectives, adverbs)

_____
_____
_____
_____

Destructive nature

Framework Objectives

W4: Learn complex polysyllabic words and unfamiliar words which do not conform to regular patterns

S10: Identify the key alterations made to a text when it is changed from an informal to a formal text

S&L11: Recognise and build on other people's contributions

Main text type: Narrative

Student Book pages 91–92

Felt-tip pens and A3 sheet will be needed.

Starter

- Reinforce some useful spelling tips, relating them to particular kinds of words. For example:
  - Polysyllabic words such as 'ob-struc-tion' are best split into syllables.
  - Prompt words that identify letter patterns are useful for remembering commonly misspelled words. (For example, the prompt word 'home' for 'women').
  - Sayings that students invent themselves can also be useful. (For example, the saying '*Fri*day is at the *end* of the week' is useful for spelling the word 'friend'.)

Introduction

Focus on: Change of style

- Read the bulletin contained in *The Birds* extract with the class. Discuss the gist of it and any unknown vocabulary, then ask students to complete **Worksheet 4.6** in pairs. They should be able to contrast the bulletin with a narrative text. Each pair should decide who will record notes in the table and who will report back. Finally, bring the class together and go through the features that pairs have identified.
- Return to the text in the Student Book (page 91); elaborate on this explanation using students' feedback from **Worksheet 4.6**. Also explain the difference between the active and the passive tenses (discussed in detail in **Unit 3**) using the 'Grammar for reading' box. Finally, work through questions **8**, **9** and **10** as a class.

Development

Key Speaking and Listening

- As part of their discussion in question **11**, students may or may not pick up the mood of the story in so far as it affects the main character and his family. They may assume, for example, that the hero will survive, although the implication is that this is unlikely. Each group should address the bulleted questions as listed on page 92 and come to their own conclusions. Encourage them to ask further questions.
- Ensure students are sufficiently well-organised in their groups so that the exploratory talk can take place within a certain time limit (ten minutes). Groups will need to appoint a recorder, a spokesperson to report to their paired group, and a chairperson who can control the discussion time.
- Each group will need a felt-tip pen and a large (preferably A3) piece of paper on which to record their conclusions. Once they have addressed each question satisfactorily, the recorder should summarise the group's findings using bullet points or numbers.

Plenary

- Bring the groups together to assess their outcomes and how they arrived at them. Ask each spokesperson to describe their group's view and whether their partner group shared it. Collate the main points on the board. Once you have these for the first group, other groups need only report on additional points that were made.

Unit 4 Destructive nature

Worksheet 4.6: What's the difference?

Use the table below to record the features of both texts from pages 86–87 in your textbook. Find the differences between them.

	Narrative text	**Official bulletin**
What is it for?		
Where would you find it?		
Who would write it?		
Formal or informal style?		
Plain or imaginative language?		
Specialised vocabulary?		
Tense and person (viewpoint)?		
Mainly factual information?		

Destructive nature

Lesson 7

Assessment Focus

AF2: Produce texts which are appropriate to task, reader and purpose
Main text type: Information

Student Book pages 93–95

Starter

- Remind students of the terms 'general' and 'specific' in relation to information texts. Then write the following on the board:
  - *Scientists think waterspouts (tornadoes) may be the cause of disappearing ships and aircraft. For example, in 1945, five US planes went missing without trace in the Bermuda Triangle.*
  Ask students which phrase precedes the specific information ('For example...').

Introduction

Stage 1
- Encourage students to make their leaflet 'reader-friendly'. Ask them what the main purposes of the leaflet will be and encourage them to think beyond 'giving information' or 'advice'. For example, one purpose could be easy access to information.
- Students should first consider the usefulness of including visual information before planning their layout. Then remind them of their work during the Starter and take them through the notes on page 94 of the Student Book. They then write their first paragraph.

Stage 2
- Go through the storm cellar notes with students and make sure they start their next section with a clear subheading.
- Students who have difficulty organising their text may find **Worksheet 4.7** helpful; it acts as a visual prompt. They can refer to it when thinking spatially about how much text to write and where to position it on the leaflet; they can also refer to it when writing. However, you should ensure that students include substantial paragraphs of text, as well as visuals or factfile boxes.

Development

Stage 3
- Students begin a full draft of their leaflet, referring to their plans and the bulleted reminders on page 95. Remind them to include general information and specific examples in their sentences.

Challenge
- Students with the time or ability may wish to turn some of their information on storm cellars into advice, using imperatives.

Peer Assessment

- When they have finished their drafts, students work in pairs to assess each other's work. Write the following features on the board and ask students to check if their drafts include them:
  - well-planned layout that aids reading
  - general points made
  - examples given
  - present and past tenses used.
- Students then complete the Peer Assessment Sheet (see page 6) and feed back.
- Students redraft according to suggestions, if possible using ICT.

Plenary

- Give a copy of **OHT 4.8** (top half only) to each group and get students to annotate the level 3 writing to show how well the student has produced a text appropriate to task, reader and purpose, and what needs improvement. Students should think particularly about the use of connectives to extend sentences. Then display the whole of **OHT 4.8** and ask for feedback on how to get the level 3 writing up to level 4. Show in the exemplar of level 4 how this can be done. Students make changes to their own texts in light of this.

Unit 4 Destructive nature

Worksheet 4.7: Leaflet planner

Use this planning frame to organise the different elements in your leaflet before you start writing.

1 Think of titles for headings and subheadings you will use and record them in each box.

2 Add short notes in each box as a reminder of:

- the information you will include
- the tense you will write in
- the illustrations, maps or diagrams (if any) you will include.

The first box has been started for you.

Remember, this is only a plan. You can change it as you write if you so wish.

Title of leaflet
_____

Introduction
General information on what tornadoes are like (see notes):
_____
_____
_____

Tenses I will write in:
_____

Illustrations, maps or diagrams to include:
_____
_____

Title of subheading:
_____
Other information:
_____
_____
_____
Tenses I will write in:
_____
Illustrations, maps or diagrams to include:
_____
_____

Title of subheading:
_____
Other information:
_____
_____
_____
Tenses I will write in:
_____
Illustrations, maps or diagrams to include:
_____
_____

Impact English Teacher's Resource © HarperCollins Publishers 2005

Unit 4 Destructive nature

OHT 4.8: Raising the level

Assessment Focus

AF2: Produce texts which are appropriate to task, reader and purpose

Level 3

Sometimes people hear there is a 'warning'. This means there is storm coming. Then people get into their storm cellars quickly. Sometimes people hear there is a 'watch'. This means a storm may be coming.

People keep useful things in a storm cellar. They keep tins of food, water, a torch, a radio and a first-aid box. The radio means they can find out what is going on.

Level 4

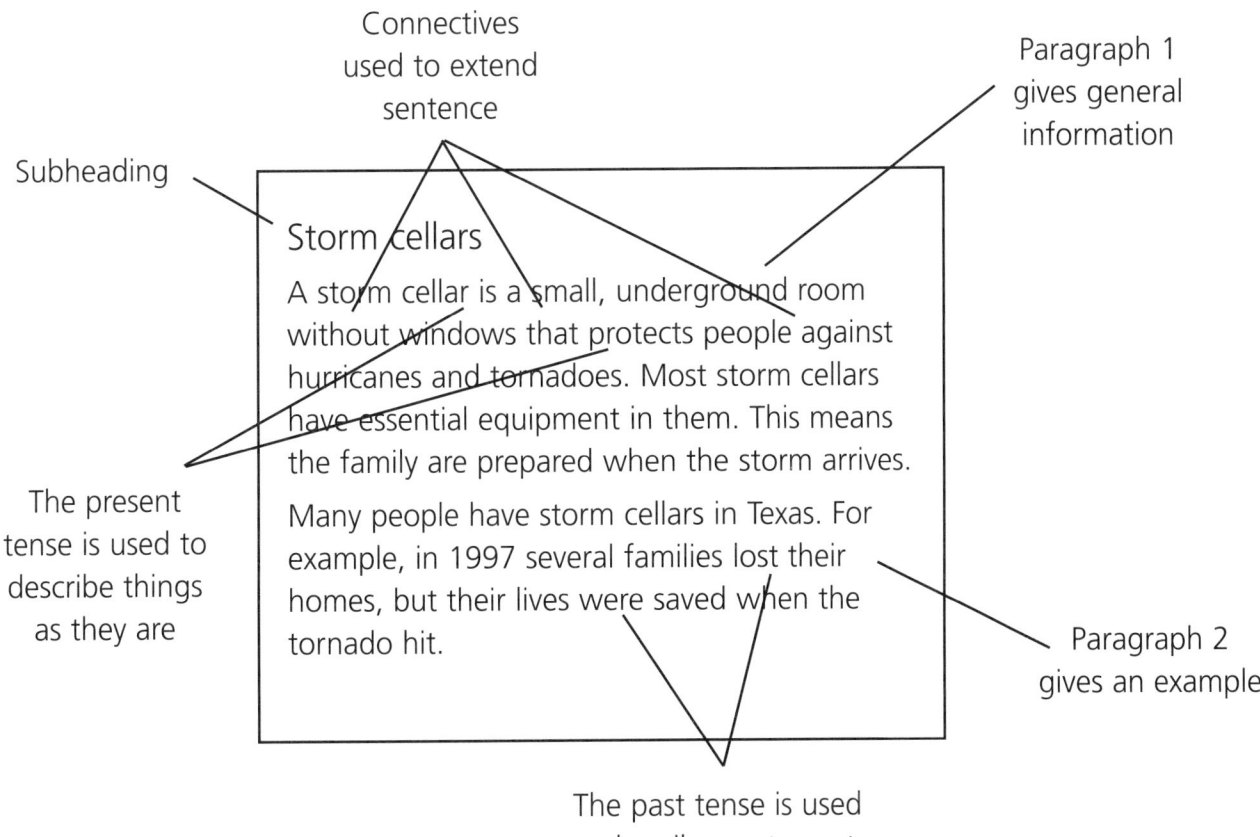

Impact English Teacher's Resource © HarperCollinsPublishers 2005

Family drama

Lesson 1

Framework Objectives

W7b: Work out the meaning of unknown words

S&L14: Develop the dramatic techniques that enable students to create and sustain a variety of roles

Main text type: Film script

Student Book pages 96–100

Starter

- Ask students what the words 'interior' and 'exterior' mean. Prompt them to look at the prefixes ('int–' and 'ext–') and ask what they think they mean. Does anyone know what the adjectives connected to both these terms are ('internal' and 'external')?
- Next, encourage students to come up with similar sounding prefixes, such as 'inter', which means 'across' or 'between'. Point out that 'interior' is a noun meaning 'the inside'.

Introduction

- Read the film script with the class. Draw attention to the use of 'EXT.' and 'INT.' and the general layout of the script.

Key Reading

- Go through the key features of film scripts as described in the text-type box on page 98. Check students' understanding by asking:
  - *Why would a producer or film director find 'EXT.' and 'INT.' helpful in a film script?*
  - *The dialogue sentences are often shortened. What is the full sentence for 'This your first time?'*
- Ask pairs to work through questions **1** to **4**. Students may need to be shown another example of visual information before they complete question **4**. Ask pairs to feed back and invite the class to comment.

Development

Purpose

- Aid students with question **5** by modelling how the lines could be read. Read Billy's first line softly; then Dad's second line louder, with voice raised. Suggest students try stressing individual words or phrases. Students then try reading the lines in pairs.
- Students work through questions **6** and **7** in the same pairs. It may help to model the gesture before they begin. Ask 2 or 3 pairs to share their performances with the class.

Reading for meaning

- Use **OHT 5.1** to help students answer question **8**. Explain the evidence supplied for the first example. Then, as a class, jointly complete the second row of the table. Students find the remaining items of evidence on their own and then feed back. Share answers as a class by adding to the OHT.
- Before students tackle question **9**, check their understanding of pronouns by asking what other pronouns they know (for example, *you, it, they, our*). Reiterate how using 'we', 'our' and 'us' reflects the audience's perspective.

Plenary

- Ask 2 or 3 students to share their scene directions – do any sound like professional scriptwriters? Elicit the idea that they, as 'actors', control some of the dramatic process. Ask them:
  - *What different ways did you play Billy and his father in today's lesson?*
  - *What different choices did you make?*

Impact English Teacher's Resource © HarperCollinsPublishers 2005

Unit 5 Family drama

OHT 5.1: Billy and his father

What the reader finds out	Evidence
Billy's father does not have much money.	Billy's father takes his wife's jewellery to the pawnshop.
Billy's father still finds it difficult to accept that Billy likes dancing.	
Billy's father doesn't have much experience of travel.	
Billy is very different from the other boys at the audition.	

Unit 5 — Family drama — Lesson 2

Framework Objective

S&L16: Collaborate in, and evaluate, the presentation of dramatic performances, scripted and unscripted, which explore character, relationships and issues

Main text type: Film script

Student Book page 101

Starter

- Ask students whether they, or anyone they know, says 'Talk proper' or 'Walk normal'? If they do, they probably don't think about it since it is acceptable amongst friends and family as informal, chatty speech. However, in written work these phrases would need to be expressed more formally. 'Proper' is an adjective; ask how 'Talk proper' or 'Walk normal' should change (using the adverbs 'properly' and 'normally'). Finally, ask students to identify which of these informal lines appears in the script on pages 96–97 of the Student Book and who says it.

Introduction

Focus on: Creating dramatic performances

- As a class, recap what happens in the *Billy Elliot* extract and the initial impressions that students have gained about Billy and his father. Ask students to reread the last section of the script to themselves, as directed in the first part of question **10**.
- Working on their own, students can then use **Worksheet 5.2** to make notes on the characters. Remind them to consider:
  - voice: pace, loudness and tone (for example, *trembling*)
  - gestures: for example, *hand raised*, *a friendly smile*
  - pauses
  - space: how close one character is to another; where each character is placed. (If necessary, demonstrate this by working with one student as a 'dummy/model' – for example, *Billy standing some way back from the desk as though scared*).

  Students should make their own judgements at this point, so stress there is to be no sharing of ideas.
- Students then move into small groups and agree how each of the characters should be played. Each group will need a blank copy of **Worksheet 5.2** (an extended version of the table on page 101 of the Student Book), to record the group's decisions.

Development

Key Speaking and Listening

- In question **11a**, groups rehearse and then perform the script they developed in question **10**. To save time, suggest that students need not act out Billy and his father climbing the stairs. They can go directly from the end of the dialogue with the receptionist ('Thanks') to Billy going into the changing room.

Plenary

- Ask students to comment on their performance and those of their group, using the bullets in question **11b** as prompts. They should focus in particular on how well the different characters were portrayed.
- Question **12**, in which students are asked to write a short commentary of their group's performance, can be set as a homework task once students have compared their group's performance with those of the other groups in the class.

Unit 5 Family drama

Worksheet 5.2: Playing characters

Complete this chart to show how you think each of the characters in the extract should behave.

For each character, consider:
- voice
- gestures and movements (including facial expressions)
- pauses
- space.

Character	What he or she is like	How this can be shown
Receptionist		
Billy		
Dad		
Simon		
John*		

* There is very little information about John so you will have to make up your own mind as to what he is like and how he behaves.

Impact English Teacher's Resource © HarperCollinsPublishers 2005

Unit 5
Family drama
Lesson 3

Framework Objectives
R5: Trace the development of themes, values or ideas in texts
R8: Investigate how meanings are changed when information is presented in different forms or transposed into different media
Main text type: Recount

Student Book pages 102–105

Starter

- Students will probably be aware of *The Simpsons* on television. Do any of them have books based on the series? Many of these books are comic-strip versions of the TV programmes. Ask students what is missing from these comic-strip versions when compared with the TV programmes (for example, *the voices and movements*). How important do students think the voices are to the series' success? Do readers of the comic strip 'hear' the different characters' voices as they read?

Introduction

- Read through the article with the class, checking that glossary words are understood. Ask 1 or 2 students to describe what the text is about.

Key Reading

- Go through the key features of recount texts as described in the text-type box on page 104. Check understanding by asking students:
  - *How do you think the writer of this article found out about Carolyn Omine, i.e. how she got the job and how she works now?* (By interviewing her.)
  - *Why isn't this article just about how she got the job? What would that omit?*
- Students work through questions **1**, **2** and **3** in pairs. During a feedback session, use question **3** to check students' understanding of how the writer uses time references to tell the reader about the different stages in Omine's life.

Development

Purpose

- Question **4** is central to students' understanding of how a text can fulfil a number of purposes. Complete the first example (finding evidence for purpose 1) as a shared class task, with you modelling the answer. If appropriate, students can then find the evidence for purpose 2 individually.

Reading for meaning

- Begin work on question **5** by looking at the article as a class and finding the reference from the example. Then ask students to go through the text and note down the other paragraphs containing references to Omine being 'a woman script writer'. In a feedback session, use **OHT 5.3** to gradually reveal the paragraphs and the highlighted references. Check whether students have found all the references. Conclude with a class discussion based on question **6** that gets students to reflect on the references they have found and infer meaning from them.

Plenary

- Open up the discussion begun in question **6** by referring students to Omine's point that boys are given more encouragement to be funny than girls. Do students think she is right? Can they think of female comedians with their own shows on television?
- Recap the two main text types included in the article (it is mainly a recount but includes some explanation).

Unit 5 Family drama

OHT 5.3: Tracing ideas

Reference 1 (paragraph 1)

When *The Simpsons* writers start to argue about storylines, one voice stands out from the rest – the only woman on the team, Carolyn Omine. But Omine admits she's not afraid to shout as loud and as hard as the boys. After three years writing for the award-winning show she's got used to fighting her corner in the testosterone-loaded atmosphere.

Reference 2 (paragraph 2)

She says: 'When I come out with a really nasty joke, I sometimes feel like I'm not the most feminine person in the world. I feel like I go back to being a girl when I get into my own office again.'

Reference 3 (paragraph 7)

Although she is the only woman writer on the show, she admits that's not rare in US TV comedy. 'In everything I've worked on I've always been the only woman, or one of two. I don't think it's about prejudice, I just think there are not so many women trying to be comedy writers.'

Reference 4 (paragraph 8)

'Only five per cent of the job is sitting writing a script. You sometimes spend 12 hours a day sitting round a table with the guys shouting over them to be heard. I don't think a lot of women would be comfortable doing that. And I think boys are encouraged far more than girls to be funny.'

Unit 5
Family drama
Lesson 4

Framework Objective

S6: Explore and compare different methods of grouping sentences into paragraphs of continuous text that are clearly focused and well developed

Main text type: Recount

Student Book pages 106–107

Starter

- Ensure students are clear what a sentence is by asking them to define its features:
  - it tends to have a complete meaning/sense on its own
  - it has a subject and a main verb
  - it starts with a capital letter and ends with a full stop.
- Then write these examples on the board and check that students understand that:
  - 'Writing for *The Simpsons* is very much…' is not a sentence (it has no subject: it doesn't say or refer to who is doing the writing; it is incomplete; it doesn't make sense).
  - 'For *The Simpsons*' is not a sentence (it has no verb).

Introduction

Focus on: Organising sentences in paragraphs

- Check that students know how many sentences are in the selected extract for question **7**. Then, using **OHT 5.4**, complete question **8**. Ask students what difference is made when the two sentences are swapped over (in the second version, the final sentence now sounds like a summary).
- When discussing question **9**, use the lower half of **OHT 5.4** to show the effect of the final sentence of the extract being moved to the beginning. Whilst looking at the OHT, ask:
  - *Do you know what 'show' is being referred to?*
  - *Do you know who 'she' is?*
  - *Would this reorganised version work as the first paragraph of the article?*
- Elicit from the class that not all paragraphs where a general point is backed up by specific details can be swapped easily without changing the sense.

Development

Key Writing

- To complete question **10**, students select two of the sentences from the four listed and construct their own short paragraph. The aim is to imitate the style of the paragraph in question **8** (a general idea followed by further details). However, students should be aware that to create the best paragraph they will need to look for links between the two sentences. They may also want to change words to make the two sentences flow better – encourage them to experiment with different pairings (examples are given in the Plenary).

Plenary

- Students share their completed paragraphs with the class. The better ones are as follows:
  - *The Simpsons* is an incredibly popular show. Millions of people around the world tune in every week to watch *The Simpsons*.
  - People will do anything to watch *The Simpsons*. Some people never miss an episode and have even cancelled weddings to catch a new one!
- Ask students why these combinations work well (because the first sentence sets up the main idea whilst the second sentence develops it and gives further details). You may wish to ask how each sentence can be improved. For example, in the first sentence pair, an improvement would be to change *The Simpsons* in the second sentence to the pronoun 'it'.

Unit 5 Family drama

OHT 5.4: Swapping sentences

1 Consider how changing the sentence order in the following paragraph changes the emphasis.

Version 1

Writing for *The Simpsons* is very much a team effort. Scripts are put together eight months before the show is screened but there's a lot of tinkering after that and changes are made right up to the last minute to ensure each episode is topical.

Version 2

Scripts are put together eight months before the show is screened but there's a lot of tinkering after that and changes are made right up to the last minute to ensure each episode is topical. Writing for *The Simpsons* is very much a team effort.

2 Now look at the effect of changing the sentence order in the following paragraph. Does the new paragraph (Version 2) make sense?

Version 1

When *The Simpsons* writers start to argue about storylines, one voice stands out from the rest – the only woman on the team, Carolyn Omine. But Omine admits she's not afraid to shout as loud and as hard as the boys. After three years writing for the award-winning show she's got used to fighting her corner in the testosterone-loaded atmosphere.

Version 2

After three years writing for the award-winning show she's got used to fighting her corner in the testosterone-loaded atmosphere. When *The Simpsons* writers start to argue about storylines, one voice stands out from the rest – the only woman on the team, Carolyn Omine. But Omine admits she's not afraid to shout as loud and as hard as the boys.

Unit 5
Family drama
Lesson 5

Framework Objective
R6: Recognise bias and objectivity, distinguishing facts from hypotheses, theories or opinions
Main text type: Review

Student Book pages 108–112

Starter

- Check students' knowledge about what is a fact and what is an opinion by writing the following statements about the film *Spider-Man 2* on the board:
  - It's a sequel to *Spider-Man*.
  - There are many special effects.
  - It's a better film than the first one.
  - The effects are pretty amazing.
  - The acting was okay.
  - It stars Tobey Maguire.
- Ask them to identify the facts (those statements that cannot be argued with).

Introduction

- Read through the article with the class, checking that glossary words are understood. Ask 1 or 2 students to describe what the review is about.

Key Reading

- Go through the key features of review texts as described in the text-type box on page 110. Check understanding by asking students:
  - *Can you think of two simple adjectives to describe a programme you like?*
  - *Why do you think the reviewer uses the present tense about a programme she has already seen?* (To give the review more immediacy; as a preview for the viewer.)
- Students work through questions **1**, **2** and **3** in pairs. During the feedback session, use question **2** to check understanding of the first text-type feature (providing key information). To ensure that students are clear what is meant by 'key information' in a review, ask them to give further examples.

Development

Purpose

- Students can attempt to answer question **4** on their own, locating the key references. Ask them to identify the words and phrases that indicate why these are positive (good) references to the show. Then use the annotated text on **OHT 5.5** to share responses. Did students find the same references? Students can then suggest what elements of extract 2 on the OHT (a negative review) suggest it is *not* a good programme.

Reading for meaning

- Students discuss question **5** in pairs, then decide on two or three appropriate adjectives to describe Susan, inferring these from the description in the review (for example, *bossy, embarrassing, thoughtless, insensitive, stupid*).

Plenary

- Conclude with an activity designed to emphasise how simple adjectives are useful in summing up characters in a review. Draw the following spidergram on the board and ask students to suggest suitable adjectives for the characters:

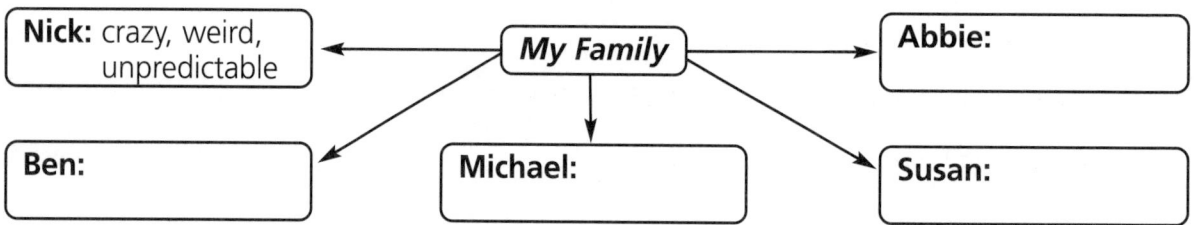

This task will be dependent on students having seen an episode of *My Family*, although it can be repeated with any other programme that students know well.

Unit 5 Family drama

OHT 5.5: Positive references

Extract 1: Analysing the references

> As we watch and laugh out loud, we can perhaps give thanks that this isn't our family, and enjoy a well-scripted and acted episode that leaves you hanging on for season five of this wonderful comedy.

- The verb phrase 'laugh out loud' suggests the viewer will agree that it is funny
- Suggests that viewers will feel thankful that it isn't their family – they will feel better because they're lucky!
- The adjective 'well-scripted' is praising the show; it doesn't say 'badly-scripted'
- Simple adjective praising the show
- This verb phrase means 'waiting impatiently', suggesting that viewers will be almost desperate to see the next series. This is praising the show, too

Extract 2: Finding the negative references

> As we watch and cover our yawns, we can perhaps wonder how this awful programme got made, and how the BBC could make the mistake of showing another series of this badly-scripted and poorly-acted so-called comedy.

My Family

Unit 5
Family drama
Lesson 6

Framework Objectives

R6: Recognise bias and objectivity, distinguishing facts from hypotheses, theories or opinions

Wr18: Write a critical review of a substantial text, taking account of the context in which it was written and the likely impact on its intended readers

Main text type: Review

Student Book pages 112–114

 Thesauruses should be available.

Starter

- The review of *My Family* uses a number of descriptions of the Harpers or individual members and their behaviour. Some are almost synonyms (for example, *bizarre* and *zany*). Check that students are familiar with the term 'synonym', then brainstorm synonyms for 'bizarre' and 'zany' (for example: *eccentric, weird, wacky*). An opposite (introduce the term 'antonym') of zany could be *dull*. Brainstorm synonyms for 'dull' (for example, *tedious, lifeless, boring*) or make thesauruses available for students to look them up. Point out that having a range of synonyms and antonyms available can be very useful in reviews, to avoid repeating the same descriptive words.

Introduction

Focus on: Recognising bias and objectivity

- Introduce the notion of bias. Usually the term 'bias' is used to describe the unfair treatment or description of someone or something, based on ignoring or selecting the facts. However, bias can also be positive when used to persuade others of your view. Ask students:
  - *When might someone use bias or be biased?*
  - *Can you give examples of people being biased against you?*
- Note that in one sense it is the duty of a reviewer to be biased – their opinion is a key reason why reviews are read and if it is too balanced or objective, the review can become boring. Point out that it is particularly difficult to be neutral about comedy. Pairs then complete question **6**, which should reinforce this point.
- Afterwards, conduct a brief plenary to collect ideas on contrasting views of comedy from 2 or 3 pairs. Model for students that it is usually possible to spot bias through:
  - the facts that are selected, for example, saying 'Henry scored a goal' equals 'he is a good player' (he may have missed ten other chances)
  - the use of loaded language around a fact, for example, '*Talented* Henry scored the best goal of the season.'
- In question **7**, pairs analyse the two reviews to identify the factual objective language in one, versus the loaded biased language in the other. Ask 1 or 2 pairs to feed back with examples of the negative bias in review 2.

Development

Key Writing

- Students now attempt question **8**, trying to avoid adjectives that suggest a viewpoint in their first paragraph (**8a**) and ensuring that their language choices in their second paragraph (**8b**) make their views clear. Remind students to use a range of adjectives including synonyms in paragraph 2. They can use *Billy Elliot* or a film of their own choice as the basis of their review.
- Students who require further support in organising the two paragraphs can arrange cut-out versions of the sample sentences on **Worksheet 5.6** as their starting point.

Plenary

- Ask 1 or 2 students to read out their reviews and invite the class to comment on their language choices.

Unit 5 Family drama

Worksheet 5.6: Planning your paragraphs

Billy Elliot is about a boy from Newcastle who wants to be a ballet-dancer.

We all know what it is like to argue with someone in your family, and the film shows this very powerfully indeed.

The story is very interesting, as it shows what it is like to fight for what you want.

Eventually, he goes to London for an audition at the Royal Ballet School.

Moreover, the characters are extremely believable, especially Billy's father who is half-ashamed and half-proud of him.

But his family don't have much money, and his father and brother don't approve of Billy's dancing.

A woman called Mrs Wilkinson coaches Billy, and persuades his family to let him apply for a place at Ballet School.

Unit 5 Assignment

Unit 5

Family drama

Lesson 7

Assessment Focus
AF2: Produce texts which are appropriate to task, reader and purpose
Main text type: Review

Student Book pages 115–117

Starter

- Write the following on the board and challenge students to match the sentences (A, B and C) to the three types of text or media (1, 2 and 3).
    A: 'Grab this fab CD right now and chill out to its lazy groove.'
    B: 'The CD has some well-crafted melodies and no doubt will be bought by the band's many fans.'
    C: 'Yeah, it's ok, I guess, but y'know, I'm just gonna download the best tracks onto my iPod.'

    1: Student talking to a friend on his mobile phone.
    2: A review in Smash Hits.
    3: A review in The Daily Telegraph.
  You could ask students how they made their choices from the language used.

Introduction

Stage 1

- Introduce the task and give out **Worksheet 5.7**. This will help students to record some basic content on which to base their preview. However, some students will not have any real performance to describe – suggest that they preview a film or drama they have seen on television. Point out that although they are writing for a local newspaper, these often review films on release nationwide.

Stage 2

- Using their notes from Stage 1, students now plan what will go into each paragraph, using the writing plan provided. Work with a guided group to ensure that students follow their plans and deliver the different focus of each paragraph. Share good examples within the group.

Development

Stage 3

- Students begin writing. They should focus on maintaining the appropriate style for the purpose of the preview. They have already decided what their viewpoint is, so their language choices should match that viewpoint. They must also ensure that the key factual elements of the preview are included. This is to pack in some detail, to keep the reader's interest.

Challenge

- More able students could write a review of their own performance outside the classroom in a play or concert, or during group work in class if they have not participated in one of these. Ask them to draft the review, using the bulleted guidance points,

Peer Assessment

- When students have finished their previews, they work in pairs to read each other's drafts. Write up the text-type features listed below and ask them to check if their drafts include them:
  - key information on both the characters and the story
  - the use of the present tense (in the main)
  - the opinion of the reviewer, expressed using adjectives or adjective + adverb combinations
  - a final summary paragraph.
- Students then complete the Peer Assessment Sheet (see page 6) and report back.
- Students redraft according to suggestions.

Plenary

- Give a copy of **OHT 5.8** (top half only) to each group and get students to annotate the level 3 writing to show whether the student has produced a text appropriate to task, reader and purpose, and what needs improvement. Then display the whole of **OHT 5.8** and ask for feedback on how to get level 3 writing up to level 4. Show in the exemplar of level 4 how this can be done. Students then make changes to their own texts in light of this.

Unit 5 Family drama

Worksheet 5.7: Making notes

Use this sheet to make notes on the show you are previewing. There is no need to write in full sentences.

Name or description of the show or performance	
When and where it is on	
Who is in it	
What happens in it (the main story/facts)	
Words that shown your opinion of the performance and the people in it. (Pack in as much detail as possible, using adverb + adjective phrases.)	
A statement summing up what you thought of it overall	

Unit 5 — Family drama

OHT 5.8: Raising the level

Assessment Focus
AF2: Produce texts which are appropriate to task, reader and purpose

Level 3

Ridgeway School's show has Simon Larwood as Tony and Lia Iqbal as Maria. It's about a boy and a girl and these gangs. It happens in New York. They fall in love but their friends are dead against it. It's okay I suppose. The dancing is okay. It was pretty good on the costumes and the singing was fantastic. I told all my mates to go but they didn't like it. So don't go.

Level 4

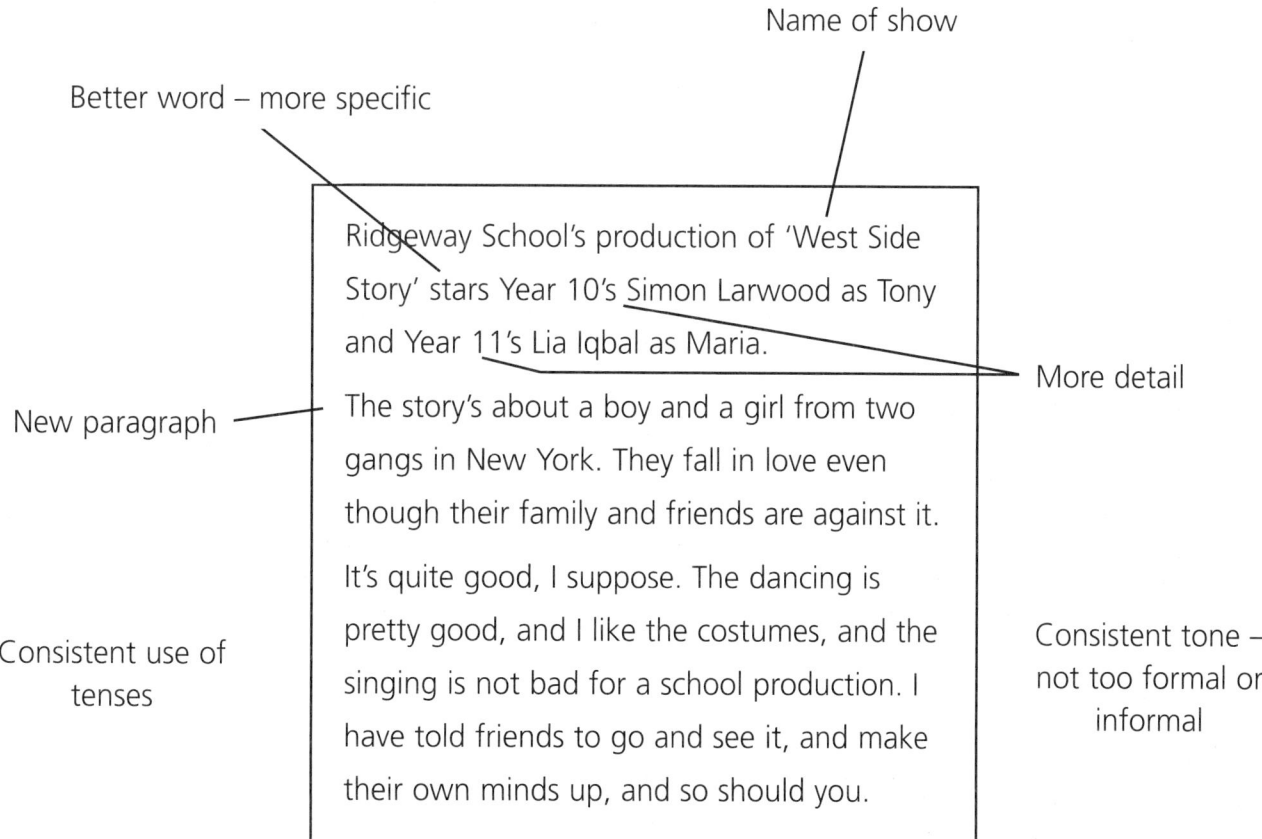

Name of show

Better word – more specific

Ridgeway School's production of 'West Side Story' stars Year 10's Simon Larwood as Tony and Year 11's Lia Iqbal as Maria.

The story's about a boy and a girl from two gangs in New York. They fall in love even though their family and friends are against it.

It's quite good, I suppose. The dancing is pretty good, and I like the costumes, and the singing is not bad for a school production. I have told friends to go and see it, and make their own minds up, and so should you.

New paragraph

Consistent use of tenses

More detail

Consistent tone – not too formal or informal

Unit 6
Refugees
Lesson 1

Framework Objectives
W1: Investigate lexical patterns in new vocabulary
R5: Trace the development of themes, values or ideas in texts
Main text type: Narrative

Student Book pages 118–122

 A map of the world should be available.

Starter

- Explain to the class that patterns are a key part of language and that many writers use patterns of words, incidents or ideas to give added depth to their work. Tell students that they are going to look at patterns within words to begin with. Then hand out **Worksheet 6.1**, in which students are asked to identify three different spelling patterns and group words accordingly.

Introduction

- Read through the extract from *Refugee Boy* with the class, checking that glossary words are understood. Use a world map to show students where Ethiopia and Eritrea are. At first, they may well assume that Chapter 2 is a mistake, as on a casual reading it might appear to be identical to the first chapter, so establish that the two chapters are set in different countries.

Key Reading

- Go through the key features of narrative texts as outlined in the text-type box on page 120. Check understanding by asking these questions:
  - *Who is the narrator of this story?*
  - *What do you think might be the crisis and ending of the story?*
  - *Which words or phrases create an atmosphere of fear?*
- Students discuss questions **1** to **4** in pairs. Invite 1 or 2 pairs to feed back for the class to comment on.

Development

Purpose

- In question **5**, students look at possible purposes for story openings and choose which one is the main purpose of the *Refugee Boy* extract.

Reading for meaning

- Following on from their answer to question **5**, students look at how a dramatic effect is created by the similarity between Chapter 1 and Chapter 2. Point out to them the way in which patterns can emphasise small differences. Students then discuss questions **6** and **7** in pairs. After a brief feedback session, they analyse the key differences between the two chapters, using a table like the one on page 122 of the Student Book (question **8**). They then consider the writer's purpose in using this repetition in question **9**. This can be done individually or
in pairs.

Plenary

- Encourage students to think about the larger implications of Zephaniah's use of repetition. What is he saying about racism?
- Ask students how many of them looked back to Chapter 1 as they read Chapter 2 to compare the two. Ask them to think about the risk that Zephaniah has taken at the beginning of the novel. Do they think there is any point at which the repetition is dull rather than effective?

Unit 6 Refugees

Worksheet 6.1: Word patterns

The words in Table 1 below fall into three different patterns. Look at them carefully and then arrange them according to the patterns you have worked out, in Table 2.

Table 1

Ancient	Receive	Deceive
Science	Believe	Conscience
Relieve	Conceive	Grieve

Table 2

Pattern 1	Pattern 2	Pattern 3

Impact English Teacher's Resource © HarperCollinsPublishers 2005

Refugees

Lesson

Framework Objectives

R5: Trace the development of themes, values or ideas in texts
S&L12: Take different roles in discussion, helping to develop ideas, seek consensus and report the main strands of thought
Main text type: Narrative

Student Book pages 122–124

Starter

- Remind students about Benjamin Zephaniah's use of repetition in the passage from *Refugee Boy*. Make sure they understand that although intentional repetition can be powerful, unintentional repetition should be avoided as it can be dull and awkward to read.

Introduction

Focus on: Patterns of language

- In this section, students move on to consider the effect of repetition *within* each chapter. Explain that part of the impact of the opening of Zephaniah's novel comes from its deliberately patterned use of language. Point out to students that the author has specifically chosen his words to create a particular effect and that it would have been perfectly possible for him to have opted for a greater variety of expressions. In question **10**, students look for examples of repetition within Chapter 1. Students work on the question in pairs, analysing the types of repetition used and the author's purpose.
- Questions **11** and **12** should also be discussed in pairs. These ask students to consider the language patterns created by the different reporting verbs and the effects these create.
- Use **Worksheet 6.2** as a follow-up exercise, to explore some of the choices that Zephaniah deliberately chose not to make.

Development

Key Writing

- Remind students of the difference between first- and third-person narratives. Read through the text on page 124 with the class. Students then discuss question **13** in pairs and feed back.
- In tackling the writing task in question **14**, more able students may be able to create some of their own language effects rather than simply repeating (or ignoring) the effects created in the original text. Briefly discuss other words for 'rifle' – for instance, the less specific word 'gun' or more specific 'AK47'. Also remind students of some of the alternative reporting verbs from **Worksheet 6.2**.

Plenary

- Ask 1 or 2 students to summarise the ways in which repetition can be both good and bad in writing. Help them, as a class, to produce a list of dos and don'ts for the use of repetition and write these on the board.

Unit 6 Refugees

Worksheet 6.2: Using 'said'

In direct speech we need to tell the reader who is speaking. The simplest way to do this is to use the word 'said'.

> For example: 'I'm here,' *said* Martin.

However if you always use 'said' it can be a little boring. This is also a chance to give your reader extra information about a character.

1 What is the difference in meaning between these two sentences?
  a 'I'm here,' announced Martin.
  b 'I'm here,' groaned Martin.

2 In pairs, discuss how you would say the two sentences above.

There are many other words that can be used instead of 'said'.

- Some tell you **what kind of statement** is being made, for example:
  added, announced, answered, asked, declared, mentioned, remarked, replied, suggested.

- Others tell you **how** a statement is made, for example:
  groaned, grunted, laughed, mumbled, muttered, screamed, shouted, whispered.

---

3 Choose the best words from the box above to fill in the gaps in these sentences.

  a 'You would like some more tea, wouldn't you?' _____ Alice.

  b 'Why do they always pick on me?' _____ Felix.

  c 'We'll be leaving in five minutes,' _____ the teacher.

  d 'That's the silliest thing I've ever heard,' _____ Adrian.

  e 'No! Don't!' _____ Iain as he fell.

Impact English Teacher's Resource © HarperCollinsPublishers 2005

Refugees

Lesson 3

Framework Objective

W10: Extend the range of connectives used to express reservations
Main text type: Information

Student Book pages 125–128

Starter

- Tell students that they are about to read a passage about asylum seekers and refugees in the UK. Ask them what they have heard about asylum seekers and refugees, or write the following on the board:
  - *They come and take the best jobs.*
  - *A lot of refugees come from countries where there's war.*
  - *People come to the UK to try and have a better life.*
  - *The UK receives over 50,000 applications for asylum every year.*
- As a class, students consider each statement, judging whether it is a fact or an opinion. Discuss the difference between fact and opinion, and, if possible, ask students to identify the source of their ideas.
- Go through the definitions of 'refugee' and 'asylum seeker' on page 126, and ensure students know the difference between them.

Introduction

- Read through the website text with the class, making sure that difficult words are understood. Referring back to the discussion in the Starter, ask students to think about the problems of sorting out fact from opinion, rumour and assumptions when discussing refugees.

Key Reading

- Go through the key features of information texts as outlined in the text-type box on page 127. Check students' understanding by asking these questions:
  - *Why is it important for an information text to be written clearly and logically?*
  - *What examples of technical language can you find?*
- Students discuss questions **1** to **3** in pairs. Students might need help with the terms in question **3**. Invite 1 or 2 pairs to feed back their answers for the class to comment on.

Development

Purpose

- Students discuss questions **4** and **5** in pairs, then feed back.

Reading for meaning

- Students use the chart in question **6** to clarify the organisation of the text – how each section starts with a comment which is then backed up by facts. They then look at the bullet-pointed section of the text more closely in question **7**.
- When they have completed the exercises, hand out **Worksheet 6.3**, which considers the use of qualifying connectives to link ideas that are not always straightforward. The worksheet could also be given as homework.

Plenary

- Discuss with students the effectiveness of the CRE website's approach. Is it merely presenting facts, or does it us other techniques as well? Ask students to compare the language used in the 'What people say' statements with 'The facts' texts.

Unit 6 Refugees

Worksheet 6.3: Using connectives

When you are dealing with facts and opinions, it is not always possible to express ideas in a simple form. Sometimes the ideas are too complicated.

Here are some of the connectives you might find in an information text:

although   unless   however   if   nonetheless

1 Practise using the connectives below by writing them in a sentence.

a however

b if

c although

d nonetheless

e unless

2 Use the words above to fill in the blanks in these sentences.

a _____ many asylum seekers are highly qualified, they often only find work in low-paid jobs.

b At first asylum seekers cost the taxpayer money, _____, in the longer term they usually put far more money into the economy than they take out.

c Asylum seekers are not permitted to work _____ they have refugee status.

d Asylum seekers can only apply for support from the National Asylum Support Service _____ they have no money of their own.

e Asylum seekers and refugees have very difficult lives; _____ some people assume they live in the lap of luxury.

Unit 6
Refugees
Lesson 4

Framework Objectives

W14: Collect and comment on examples of language change
R8: Investigate how meanings are changed when information is presented in different forms or transposed into different media
S&L3: Make a formal presentation in Standard English, using appropriate rhetorical devices
Main text type: Information

Student Book pages 129–130

Starter

- Use **OHT 6.4** to allow students to explore the language of the Internet. Work through each example with the class and write their answers on the OHT. Ask students if they can identify the ways in which new words are formed. Some of the processes involved include: new meanings for old words (thread), acronyms (URL), blending (firewall) and the use of prefixes (hyperlink).

Introduction

Focus on: Organising information on a webpage

- Remind students that the text on page 125–126 is from a website. Ask them to identify some of the advantages and disadvantages of presenting information on a webpage as opposed to leaflet form and then read through the section on scrolling on page 129. Students discuss questions **8** and **9** in pairs. They then turn to the particular design features of a webpage and consider their advantages and disadvantages (question **10** and **11**.)
- Students should consider the question of reaching a target audience. Discuss the following questions:
  - Are people who are prejudiced against asylum seekers likely to log on to the CRE's website?
  - How would campaigners who support asylum seekers use the website?
  - Could another means of communication, such as a leaflet, be more effective?

Development

Key Speaking and Listening

- For question **12**, students use the information from the CRE website to produce a formal presentation on refugees in pairs. Students should take the reminder points on page 130 into account when preparing their speeches. Help less able students to select information, and make further suggestions for visual aids where appropriate.
- As an extension task, students can access the website. If this is not possible, ask students how they would go about obtaining contact details for the CRE.

Plenary

- Ask pairs to present their speeches to the class, and invite constructive criticism.

Unit 6 Refugees

OHT 6.4: Webspeak

Language changes over time to cope with new ideas and technologies. Some language is completely new but most new words build on older ones.

Below are some words associated with the internet. For each word say what it means and then try to work out how the word was formed. The first example has been filled in for you.

Word	What it means	Where it came from
hyperlink	A link on a web page that takes you to another part of page or to a different page.	It is a combination of 'hyper' (meaning 'over' or 'across') and 'link' (something that joins two things).
Internet		
e-mail		
to google		
virus		
broadband		

Impact English Teacher's Resource © HarperCollinsPublishers 2005

Refugees

Lesson 5

Framework Objective

Wr10: Organise and present information, selecting and synthesising appropriate material and guiding the reader through the text (an information leaflet)

Main text type: Advice

Student Book pages 131–135

Starter

- Explain to students that they are going to be looking at a leaflet which gives advice on how to organise a campaign. Outline to them some of the different methods of attracting the attention of the government, such as marches, direct action and petitions, and explain that one of the simplest methods of contacting the government is by writing to your MP.

Introduction

- Read the extract from the STAR leaflet with the class, checking that difficult words are understood.

Key Reading

- Go through the key features of advice texts as outlined in the text-type box on page 133. Check understanding by asking these questions:
  – What is this advice text advising the reader to do?
  – Find another example of formal language.
- Students discuss questions **1** and **2** in pairs. Invite 1 or 2 pairs to feed back for the class to comment on.
- Make sure all students are quite clear about what an imperative verb is by going through the definition in the 'Grammar for reading' box. Students then discuss questions **3** and **4** in pairs.

Development

Purpose

- Students discuss question **5** in pairs. In order to clarify the logical organisation of an effective advice text, hand out **Worksheet 6.5**, in which students have to reorder a set of paragraphs.

Reading for meaning

- Read through this section with the class. It extends their understanding of an advice text by demonstrating how each logical point can be backed up by reasons and examples. In question **6**, students find another reason supporting the advice given in the text. In question **7**, they look for examples that expand on the main point. These questions can be done individually or in pairs

Plenary

- Invite 2 or 3 students to recap the main features of advice texts. Stress that they should give advice but also use persuasive techniques. Students could look briefly at these and discuss how the leaflet attempts to motivate its readers as well as give them advice.

Impact English Teacher's Resource © HarperCollinsPublishers 2005

Unit 6 Refugees

Worksheet 6.5: Advice leaflet

You are planning a leaflet to be given out to new Year 7 students at your school. Here are the points you have decided you need to include:

- **A** Finding your way around the school
- **B** How to cope with fellow students
- **C** An outline of the main problems
- **D** How to cope with teachers
- **E** How to cope with all the books
- **F** A summary of the best way to make sure you are happy
- **G** How to cope with the timetable.

1 Write down the most logical order for your paragraphs to go in.

_____

_____

2 What sort of language will you use?
- **a** Very informal
- **b** Very formal
- **c** A mixture of formal and informal.

3 Below are the opening sentences for all the paragraphs. Match each sentence with its corresponding paragraph. The first example has been done for you.
- **i** Using a timetable for the first time can be confusing. __G__
- **ii** Another problem you may have is carrying so many books around. _____
- **iii** How do you find the right classroom? _____
- **iv** Starting a new school can be fun, but you also may have some difficulties to begin with. _____
- **v** Despite these potential problems, we hope you will enjoy Westlake High School. _____
- **vi** Meeting new people isn't always easy. _____
- **vii** Getting to know the teachers is also important. _____

Student Action

Refugees

Lesson

Framework Objectives

S7: Develop different ways of linking paragraphs, using a range of strategies to improve cohesion and coherence

Wr15: Give written advice which offers alternatives and takes account of possible consequences

Main text type: Advice

Student Book pages 136–137

Starter

- Discuss with students what the main purpose of an advice text usually is (to advise the reader to take a particular course of action). Explain that they are going to be producing a poster to accompany the STAR leaflet. Ask students to identify the main differences between a poster and a leaflet. Write their ideas on the board for reference during the lesson. Ideas might include: *amount of text, need to be read from a distance, lack of space for an argument, need for visuals, punchy, attention-grabbing language.*

Introduction

Focus on: Formal language, informal tone

- In this section, students will explore differences in language and tone created by using formal and informal language features. Remind students of the differences between formal and informal language. Then look at the example on page 136 and go through the 'Grammar for reading' box to remind students of conditional sentences. They then produce their own sentences in question **8**. In question **9** they find examples of informal language featured in the extract.

Development

Key Writing

- Read through the instructions in question **10** to focus students on their brief. Discuss some initial ideas as a class to ensure they understand clearly what they are going to do. Hand out **Worksheet 6.6** and ask students to complete it before they start work on question **12**, to help them understand how to design an effective poster.
- Students can then start work on their posters. Make sure they use imperatives and informal language, as well as a strong image and good design features, such as a strong heading and highlighted key words.

Plenary

- Ask students to show their posters, or work in progress, and explain how they have fulfilled the design/campaign criteria. The rest of the class can give constructive criticism.

Unit 6 Refugees

Worksheet 6.6: Designing posters

1 Look carefully at the two posters on this page and annotate them to show their good and bad points. The first annotation has been done for you.

campaign logo included

2 Which of the two posters works best? Give reasons for your choice.

Impact English Teacher's Resource © HarperCollinsPublishers 2005

Refugees
Lesson 7

Assessment Focus
AF2: Produce texts which are appropriate to task, reader and purpose

Student Book pages 138–141

Starter

- Ask students to write down the main features of advice texts, then feed back to the class. Present the assignment to students as outlined in the Student Book. Make sure that they have a clear idea of their audience, as well as the format of a leaflet. Stress that they will be writing advice on how to write a letter, not the letter itself, and relate the features of advice texts as discussed to this task.

Introduction

Stage 1
- Students begin by planning the sections of their leaflet and deciding which four headings from the list on page 138 they are going to include.
- For further help with planning, use **Worksheet 6.7**. If students are using word processors, the different columns can be achieved by using a landscape page and setting the text with a two-column layout. They should think about the amount of space they have to play with as well as the content, even at the planning stage.

Development

Stage 2
- The sample letter layout should be -placed on the inside panels. Students will need to think carefully about spacing as they write. The advice should be in an appropriate style – students can refer to the notes on page 139 as they draft their work. They should be able to state clearly the purpose of each paragraph they are writing. Remind them that the choice of font can also affect the perceived level of formality of a document.

Stage 3
- Read through the reminder points on page 141 of the Student Book and ask students to redraft their leaflets where necessary.

Challenge
- Students should attempt to achieve a mixture of formal and informal language in this leaflet. Ask them to read through the 'Challenge' box and then change one or two of the imperatives in their leaflet into this more formal style.

Peer Assessment

- When students have completed their writing, they work in pairs and read each others' drafts. Write up the text-type features listed below and ask them to check if their drafts include them:
  - clear organisation
  - appropriate choice of formal or informal language
  - direct address
  - imperative verbs
  - useful layout design.
- Students fill in the Peer Assessment Sheet (see page 6) and feed back their findings.
- Students redraft according to suggestions.

Plenary

- Give each group a copy of **OHT 6.8** (top half only). Ask students to annotate the level 3 writing to show how well the student has produced a text appropriate to its purpose and what needs improvement. Then display the whole of **OHT 6.8** and ask for feedback on how to get the level 3 writing up to level 4. Show in the exemplar of level 4 how this can be done, then ask students to make changes to their own texts in light of this.

Unit 6 Refugees

Worksheet 6.7: Designing a leaflet

You are about to design a four panel leaflet using an A4 sheet of paper. Fold your A4 sheet in half so that it has the following sections:

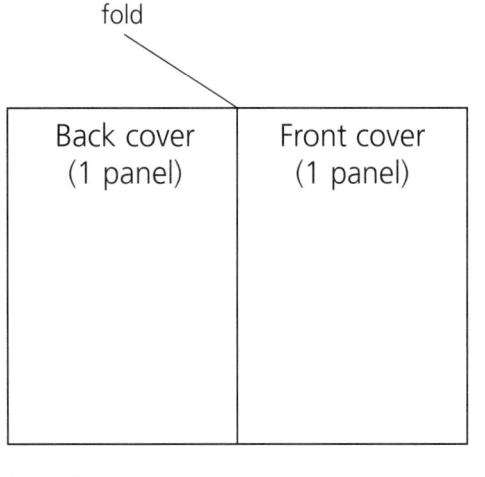

For the front cover you might like to include some or all of the following:
- An attractive type face or font
- A title
- A striking illustration
- Space for the campaign logo.

For the back cover you might choose to include:
- A summary of your main advice
- Further information such as telephone numbers.

The following also need to be included in your leaflet. Use the plan below to decide where they will go:
- Your four sections of text (see Stage 1), including an introduction and a conclusion
- The diagram on page 140 of your Student Book.

Front cover: _____
Inside 1: _____
Inside 2: _____
Back cover: _____

Remember:
- Fold the paper as neatly as you can and make sure each section is in the right place.
- Check that you have used the appropriate language and style.
- Think carefully about how your choice of font might affect how formal or informal the leaflet looks.

Unit 6 Refugees

OHT 6.8: Raising the level

Assessment Focus

AF2: Produce texts which are appropriate to task, reader and purpose

Level 3

The layout of the letter is pretty obvious. Your address goes at the top and then the date and 'Dear MP'. The first paragraph is the reason for the letter and then the next paragraph is about what should be done.

This type of letter usually has the address of the person that it is being written to above the 'Dear MP' bit.

Level 4

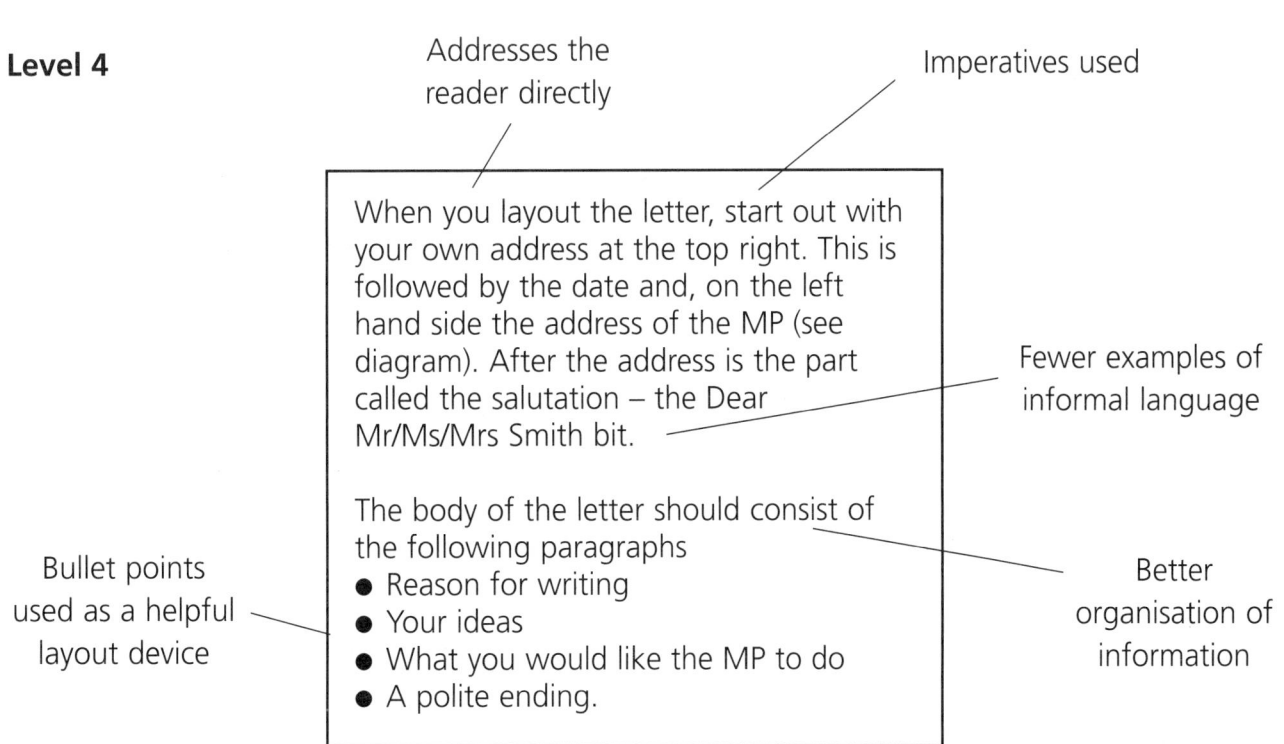

Impact English Teacher's Resource © HarperCollinsPublishers 2005

New media

Framework Objective
R9: Recognise how texts are shaped by the technology they use
Main text type: Persuasion

Student Book pages 142–146

Starter

- Are cartoons just for telling a story? Write some text types on the board (for example, *information*, *persuasion*, *explanation*, *advice*) and ask students how a cartoon could be used for these purposes. Explore in discussion what advantages a cartoon has over other forms of presenting.

Introduction

- Read through The Bug advert with the class, checking that glossary words are understood. Ask 1 or 2 students to describe what the story and the second part of the text are generally about.

Key Reading

- Go through the key features of persuasion texts as described in the text-type box on page 144. Check students' understanding by asking:
  - *What is the 'single viewpoint' of this advert?*
  - *What does 'emotive' mean?*
  - *What is 'direct address'?*
- Students discuss questions **1** to **4** in pairs. Some of them may need guidance in finding the correct part of the text in question **1**. For question **3**, a prompt about Hemingway's friendly tone may help students to decide between the bulleted options. Ask 2 or 3 pairs to feed back their answers and invite the class to comment.

Development

Purpose

- Students discuss question **5** in small groups and feed back. Ensure they understand that the main purpose of an advert is to sell something (even if that something is an idea) despite any other content (such as information and entertainment). However, students can be allowed any combination of the four options, providing they are well argued.
- Question **6** can be attempted in pairs or individually.

Reading for meaning

- Explain how you can 'read' a text in different ways – especially a persuasive text that has a hidden agenda.
- In question **7** pairs write out the story of the cartoon. When they have finished, show through the example on page 146 of the Student Book how the words, images and ideas in the cartoon can be 'read' to gather evidence for its underlying persuasive purpose. Pairs then make notes on the rest of the cartoon for question **8**. To support this activity, provide each pair with a copy of **Worksheet 7.1** on which to record their ideas and write an evaluation. Question **9** encourages students to think about how the cartoon might appear on a website (i.e. with sound and moving images).

Plenary

- Select three or four frames of the cartoon and ask students what their 'hidden message' might be. Encourage the class to add other students' comments to their tables (**Worksheet 7.1**), since they will be using these notes when writing their presentations for the 'Key Speaking and Listening' task (question **11**).

Unit 7: New media

Worksheet 7.1: Reading the cartoon

1 In pairs, discuss what the cartoon is really telling you about The Bug. Make your notes in the table below. Some examples have already been given, to start you off.

What it's telling me about the product – The Bug	*Frame 1 – it's important enough for there to be a story about its 'birth'.*
What it's telling me about the designer – Wayne Hemingway	*Frame 1 – he is famous, like a film star.* *Frame 2 – he is on our level, an ordinary person like us.*

2 Write two or three sentences saying whether you think the cartoon's 'hidden message' is effective, giving your reasons.

_____
_____
_____
_____

New media

Lesson 2

Framework Objectives

S9: Adapt the stylistic conventions of the main non-fiction text types to fit different audiences and purposes

S&L4: Provide an explanation or commentary which links words with actions or images

Main text type: Persuasion

Student Book pages 146–148

Starter

- Ask students, working in groups, to think how the technology of the Internet has affected the form of adverts. They should brainstorm how adverts on the Internet differ from those in print. Drawing on their previous work for question **9** (during which they considered the Internet version of the cartoon in the Bug advert), ask students how the web version of the whole advert would differ from the print version. If you have easy access to the Internet, log on to the website www.thebug.com and find out.

Introduction

Focus on: Suiting audience and purpose

- Read through the section, emphasising how important it is to determine the audience and purpose of a text before evaluating (or writing) it. Model the example on page 147 of the Student Book, to show how well the language and tone of the text suits the audience and purpose of The Bug advert. Recap the meanings of the terms 'emotive', 'tone', 'informal language', 'colloquialism' and 'contraction'. Students then attempt question **10**.
- To support question **10**, **Worksheet 7.2** provides a version of the extract on which students should identify and then annotate the bulleted features. Ask 2 or 3 students to present their annotations on an OHT and invite the class to comment.

Development

Key Speaking and Listening

- Outline the scenario in question **11**, explaining how businesses ask advertising agencies to come up with advertising and/or marketing ideas for their products. Pairs then draw on the work they did for questions **7** and **8** (**Worksheet 7.1**) and question **9** in order to put together an effective presentation that will 'sell' their idea of the cartoon to PURE Digital. Discuss with the class how pairs might divide up their responsibilities (question **11b**) and how they could make their presentations persuasive (question **11c**).
- Emphasise to students the fact that their presentation is a persuasive spoken text, just as the advert is a persuasive written text. Remind them of the main features of persuasive texts by referring students back to the text-type features on page 144 of the Student Book. Put students in groups of 4 instead of pairs, if necessary, to suit either higher or lower abilities.

Plenary

- Ask 2 or 3 pairs to make their presentations to the class. The rest of the class could act as the management board of PURE Digital and ask questions at the end of the presentation; pairs or groups then respond to clarify points. Invite the class to comment both on the content of the presentations and the persuasive techniques used.

Unit 7: New media

Worksheet 7.2: Audience and purpose

In pairs, make notes on the extract below to show how the language of the advert is suited to its audience and purpose. You need to look out for the following features:

- **Informal language** – colloquialisms, contractions.
- **Emotive language** – words or punctuation to make you feel a certain way.
- **Tone** – being cool, funny or friendly.
- **Direct address** – to make the text personal to you.

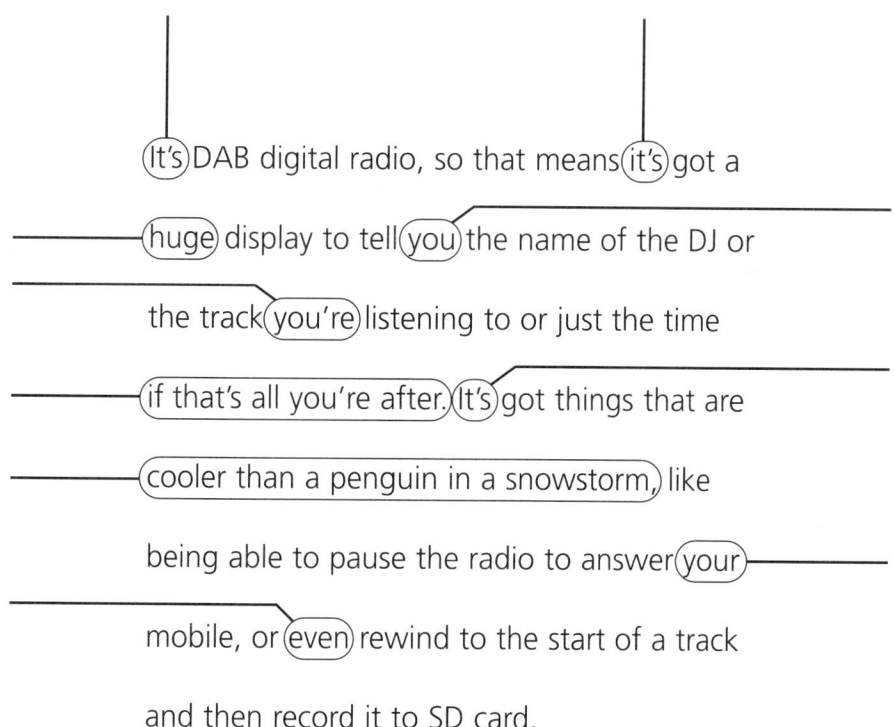

It's DAB digital radio, so that means it's got a huge display to tell you the name of the DJ or the track you're listening to or just the time if that's all you're after. It's got things that are cooler than a penguin in a snowstorm, like being able to pause the radio to answer your mobile, or even rewind to the start of a track and then record it to SD card.

New media

Lesson 3

Framework Objective
W14: Collect and comment on examples of language change
Main text type: Argument

Student Book pages 149–152

📖 Dictionaries should be available.

Starter

- Explore different ways in which new words are formed, using categories from **Worksheet 7.3**. (Revisit the meanings of 'prefix' and 'suffix', if necessary). Put some example words up on the board (such as *hairbrush, unpack, exam, buff, igloo*). Put students in pairs and hand out a set of cards from **Worksheet 7.3** to each pair. Their task is to match the words to the different categories, using a dictionary. If appropriate, reduce the number of examples from each category from two to one.

Introduction

- Read the article aloud with the class, checking that glossary words are understood. Ask students to describe what it is about.

Key Reading

- Go through the key features of argument texts as shown in the text-type box on page 151. Check students' understanding by asking:
  - *What do we mean by evidence?*
  - *What is formal language?*
  - *What does 'signposting' an argument mean?*
- Students attempt questions **1** to **4** in pairs. Students may need help unpicking the image in question **3**; you may need to explain that the M25 has traffic jams even outside of rush hours. Ask 2 or 3 pairs to feed back their answers and invite the class to comment.

Development

Purpose

- Read through the text on the purpose of an argument text, emphasising how an argument is made up of a series of step-by-step points. Highlight where the points 'in favour' of the Internet are made in the article (in paragraphs 1 and 2) and model the note-like summaries provided for these on page 152. (Accept that these points are not really 'in favour', if students point this out, but do not go into this in detail at this stage.)
- For question **5**, pairs identify and summarise the 'points against' the Internet in the final three paragraphs of the article. When they feed back, ask students to evaluate how effective these points are.

Plenary

- Elicit from students the four key features of argument texts:
  - a series of points in logical order
  - points backed up by evidence or reasons
  - formal language
  - clear signposting.
  Students should not refer to their textbooks.

Unit 7 New media

Worksheet 7.3: New word origins

Combining two words	britpop
	spin doctor
Adding a prefix or suffix to a word	teleshopping
	Internet
Using part of an existing word	phone
	disco
Giving a new meaning to an old word	hacker
	mobile
Taking a word from another language	hamburger
	shampoo
Naming after a person, place or product	bikini
	Walkman

Unit 7
New media
Lesson 4

Framework Objectives

R7: Identify the ways implied and explicit meanings are conveyed in different texts

Wr14: Develop and signpost arguments in ways that make the logic clear to the reader

Main text type: Argument

Student Book pages 152–155

Starter

- Write the following sentence on the board: *Yeah, you're an ace footballer!* Brainstorm with the class what this sentence could mean, then raise the idea of the context helping the meaning. Remove the 'Yeah' from the sentence and ask whether this makes one meaning more likely than another. Then add 'laughed Greg' to the end of the sentence and ask whether this makes one meaning more likely than another. Introduce the terms 'explicit meaning' and 'implied meaning', using the 'Grammar for reading panel' on page 153 of the Student Book. Invite students to come up with further examples of explicit and implied meanings.

Introduction

Reading for meaning

- Model the example from the article (on page 152 of the Student Book), reinforcing the work previously done on the terms 'explicit' and 'implied' and introducing the concept of irony. It may help students if you link irony with sarcasm, explaining that the former is an extended and sophisticated form of the latter.
- Pairs then draw up and complete the table in question **6**, as outlined for paragraphs 1 and 2 of the article. Alternatively, pairs can be given copies of **Worksheet 7.4**. This identifies all the examples of irony from paragraphs 1 and 2, allowing pairs to concentrate on the possible meanings.
- After a feedback session, discuss with the class whether the writer's use of irony is effective.

Development

Focus on: Signposting arguments

- Explain the idea of clear signposting in texts and ask students why this is especially important in argument texts.
- Use the annotated example from the article (on page 154 of the Student Book) to show how the signpost 'All it does' helps the reader to understand where the argument is going. Contrast this example with a sentence starting 'It makes information more easily available'. Explain also that signposts can be simple connectives such as 'but' or 'however', as well as phrases. Students then analyse the signposting in the next sentence for question **7**, working on their own or in pairs, and feed back.

Key Writing

- Students attempt question **8** in pairs or on their own (in which case they should peer review their sentences with a partner). Remind them to draw on their previous work on signposting sentences to devise a range of ways to link the two sentences. Finally, ask 2 or 3 pairs to read out their new sentences and invite the class to comment.

Plenary

- Explain to students that they are going to write a mini-argument. First, ask them to write down one sentence saying whether this lesson has been useful. They then add a sentence backing up their main point. Invite feedback from several students and ask the class to comment on how well each student has signposted his or her argument. What kinds of signpost have been used?

110

Impact English Teacher's Resource © HarperCollinsPublishers 2005

Unit 7 New media

Worksheet 7.4: Analysing irony

Working in pairs, read the table below. In column 1, examples of irony have been provided from the first two paragraphs of the newspaper article. Your task is to complete columns 2 and 3 of the table by writing down the explicit and the implied meaning for each example.

A few examples have already been provided, to start you off.

Sentence	Explicit meaning	Implied meaning
'This is the latest headline in a long list of wonderful things…'	The Internet can do lots of wonderful things.	The things the Internet does aren't that wonderful.
'There are e-bookshops where you can buy…'	You can even buy books on the Internet.	But only to help you solve the problems the Internet causes in the first place.
'There are virtual jobs in virtual offices…'	You can work from home using the Internet.	
'Suddenly the Internet is the solution to everything.'		
'The Prime Minister is lying awake at night…'		
' "Have you thought about looking on the Internet?" says Cherie.'		
'And there it is, instantly available – and all for the price of a local phone call.'		
'The way to end world poverty, the secret of eternal happiness, the cure for cancer…'		
'…apparently you can find out something about almost anything by logging on to the Internet.'		

Impact English Teacher's Resource © HarperCollinsPublishers 2005

New media

Lesson 5

Framework Objective

S4: Explore the effects of changes in tense
Main text type: Recount

Student Book pages 156–160

Starter

- Remind the class how regular verbs in english form the past tense, by writing examples on the board, for example walk, walked; hate, hated. Then explain that many verbs in english do not follow this pattern; ask for some examples. Put **OHT 7.5** up and ask the class to identify which past tenses in the poem are correct, and which are not (they will soon recognise the pattern). What are the correct past tenses in each case?

Introduction

- Read through the article with the class, checking that glossary words are understood. Ask questions about the topic of the article, to check students' understanding.

Key Reading

- Go through the key features of recount texts as described in the text-type box on page 158. Check understanding by asking students:
  - Why do recount texts mainly use the past tense?
  - Can you think of another phrase that means 'in time order'?
  - What job do time connectives do?
- Students discuss questions **1** to **4** in pairs. You may want to prompt students in question **2** about why the present tense has been used at the start of the text; explain that this is quite common in recount texts that shift from current to past events. When answering question **3**, check that students use their knowledge of time order to scan the text in the right direction. Finally, ask 2 or 3 pairs to feed back their answers and invite the class to comment.

Development

Purpose

- Pairs discuss the options in question **5**. Encourage students to rule out the clearly inappropriate reasons and find the evidence for the remaining options before deciding on the main reason. Pairs should be ready to feed back to the class.

Reading for meaning

- Explain the idea of 'fast rewind' by writing an example on the board and then referring to its use at the beginning of the article. The technique is a more extreme version of 'flashback'. Students then use the technique to continue two newspaper stories in question **6**.
- Next, introduce the idea of timelines as a useful way of analysing and planning a recount text. For question **7**, students map the events of the article using a timeline, then consider why some events have been amplified by the writer. Ask 1 or 2 students to share their timelines with the class.

Plenary

- Elicit from students the four key features of recount texts, without referring to their textbooks.

Unit 7 New media

OHT 7.5: The Verbs in English Are a Fright

The verbs in English are a fright –
How can we learn to read and write?
Today we speak, but first we spoke;
Some faucets leak, but never loke.
Today we write, but first we wrote;
We bite our tongues, but never bote.
Each day I teach, for years I taught,
And preachers preach, but never praught.
This tale I tell; this tale I told;
I smell the flowers, but never smold.
If knights still slay, as once they slew,
Then do we play, as once we plew?
If I still do as once I did,
Then do cows moo, as once they mid?

by R. Lederer

Unit 7
New media
Lesson 6

Framework Objective

S1: Combine clauses into complex sentences, using the comma effectively as a boundary signpost and checking for fluency and clarity

Main text type: Recount

Student Book pages 160–162

Starter

- Write the following words down the centre of the board: *can, should, will, must, could, ought to, have to, may*. Then add a verb on the right (for example, *play*), and a pronoun on the left (for example, *I*). Ask students what extra meaning is added to 'I play' when each of the words in the centre are placed in front of the verb. (For example, 'I can play' means 'I am allowed to play' or 'I am able to play'). Write these sentences on the board. Explain that these are modal verbs, which add meaning to (modify) other verbs.

Introduction

- Read through question **8** with the class. Run through the first meaning of 'have' (to 'own' or 'experience') described in the list on page 160. Since you have already explained during the Starter what a modal verb is, students should understand that this is the second meaning of 'have' described on page 160. Ask pairs to scan the article for examples of both meanings and feed back.

Development

Focus on: More effective sentences

- Read through the section with the class, ensuring that students understand what a clause is. Ask students how the conjunction 'but' relates the two clauses in the example on page 161 of the Student Book. Then draw the distinction between:
  - conjunctions such as 'but' and 'and', which generally add meaning by showing how *clauses* are linked within a sentence
  - connective phrases such as 'All this shows…', which show how *whole sentences or paragraphs* are linked.
- Pairs then attempt question **9**. It may help students' analysis if you write the two-sentence version on the board, i.e. 'Ten years later, he returned to Britain. He lived with his grandmother and younger brother.'
- To extend this work, students can investigate the effects of using different sentence types by analysing the two passages on **Worksheet 7.6**.

Key Writing

- Run through the notes on Dominic McVey with the class, explaining how he became a millionaire. In question **10**, students turn the notes into an article in continuous prose by writing full sentences and combining them in an effective way (refer students to their previous work for question **9**). Model how students could begin their written piece, using the example on page 162. Work with a guided group to help with drafting and share the best sentences.

Plenary

- Ask 2 or 3 students to read out their articles and invite the class to feed back. Students should consider the following questions:
  - *Have clauses been combined effectively?*
  - *Have connectives been used to make the connection of ideas clear between sentences?*
  - *Have the correct tenses been used?*

Unit 7 New media

Worksheet 7.6: Branson's first swim

Richard Branson, another entrepreneur, describes in his autobiography how he plunged into a river. His aunt had offered him ten shillings if he could learn to swim.

> I braced myself and jumped forward against the current, but I immediately felt myself sinking, my legs slicing uselessly through the water. The current pushed me around, tore at my underpants and dragged me downstream. I couldn't breathe and I swallowed water. I tried to reach up to the surface, but had nothing to push against. I kicked and writhed around but it was no help.
>
> Then my foot found a stone and I pushed up hard. I came back above the surface and took a deep breath. The breath steadied me, and I relaxed. I had to win that ten shillings.

Branson could have written the passage like this:

> I braced myself. I jumped forward against the current. I immediately felt myself sinking. My legs sliced uselessly through the water. The current pushed me around. It tore at my underpants. It dragged me downstream. I couldn't breathe. I swallowed water. I tried to reach up to the surface. I had nothing to push against. I kicked. I writhed around. It was no help.
>
> Then my foot found a stone. I pushed up hard. I came back above the surface. I took a deep breath. The breath steadied me. I relaxed. I had to win that ten shillings.

1. How many sentences are there in the first version? _____

2. How many sentences are there in the second version? _____

3. Is there any real difference in meaning between the two versions? _____

4. Which version looks and sounds better? Why? _____

_____

_____

_____

Impact English Teacher's Resource © HarperCollinsPublishers 2005

Unit 7 Assignment

New media

Lesson 7

Assessment Focus

AF3: Organise and present whole texts effectively, sequencing and structuring information, ideas and events

Main text type: Argument

Student Book pages 163–165

Starter

- Ask students to jot down four main features of argument texts, then share answers as a class. Present the task to the students as outlined in the Student Book (page 163) and ask them how the main features just explored relate to the specific task of writing a letter in favour of the Internet.

Introduction

Stage 1

- Read through the instructions for Stage 1. Students then work in small groups to brainstorm arguments in favour of the Internet; each group should summarise at least three main points in a spidergram. Invite 2 or 3 groups to feed back to the class, to ensure that everyone is working along the right lines.

Stage 2

- Students plan their letters using their three best points in favour of the Internet; encourage them to plan one paragraph per bullet point.
- Using an OHT of **Worksheet 7.7**, model how to use a text skeleton to organise the main points (on the left) and the supporting points (on the right). Then give a copy of **Worksheet 7.7** to each student, to help them plan their text. Finally, model the first example on page 165 as a reminder of signposting and how to back up the main points.

Development

Stage 3

- Students work on their own to produce their draft paragraphs. If necessary, remind them how to structure the layout of a formal letter (see **Unit 6** Assignment). Work with low-ability groups to share progress, deal with questions and problems, and praise achievement.

Challenge

- Encourage students who have the time or ability to use irony in their letter.

Peer Assessment

- Pairs read each other's draft letters. Write up the text-type features below and ask students to check whether their drafts include them:
  - a series of points, each backed-up with evidence
  - formal but effective language
  - the use of signposting to make arguments clear.
- Students complete the Peer Assessment Sheet (see page 6) and feed back. Also run through the second example on page 165 which shows how part of an argument has been rephrased to make it more effective.
- Students then redraft their argument according to their partner's suggestions.

Impact English Teacher's Resource © HarperCollinsPublishers 2005

Plenary

- Give a copy of **OHT 7.8** (top half only) to each group and get students to annotate the level 3 writing to show how well the student has structured their text, and what needs improving. Then display the whole of **OHT 7.8** and ask for feedback on how to get the level 3 writing up to level 4. Show in the exemplar of level 4 how this can be done.
- Share some of the completed letters.

Unit 7 — New media

Worksheet 7.7: Planning your argument

Use the text skeleton below to plan the argument for your letter. The main points are numbered on the left. Note down one or two supporting points next to each main point.

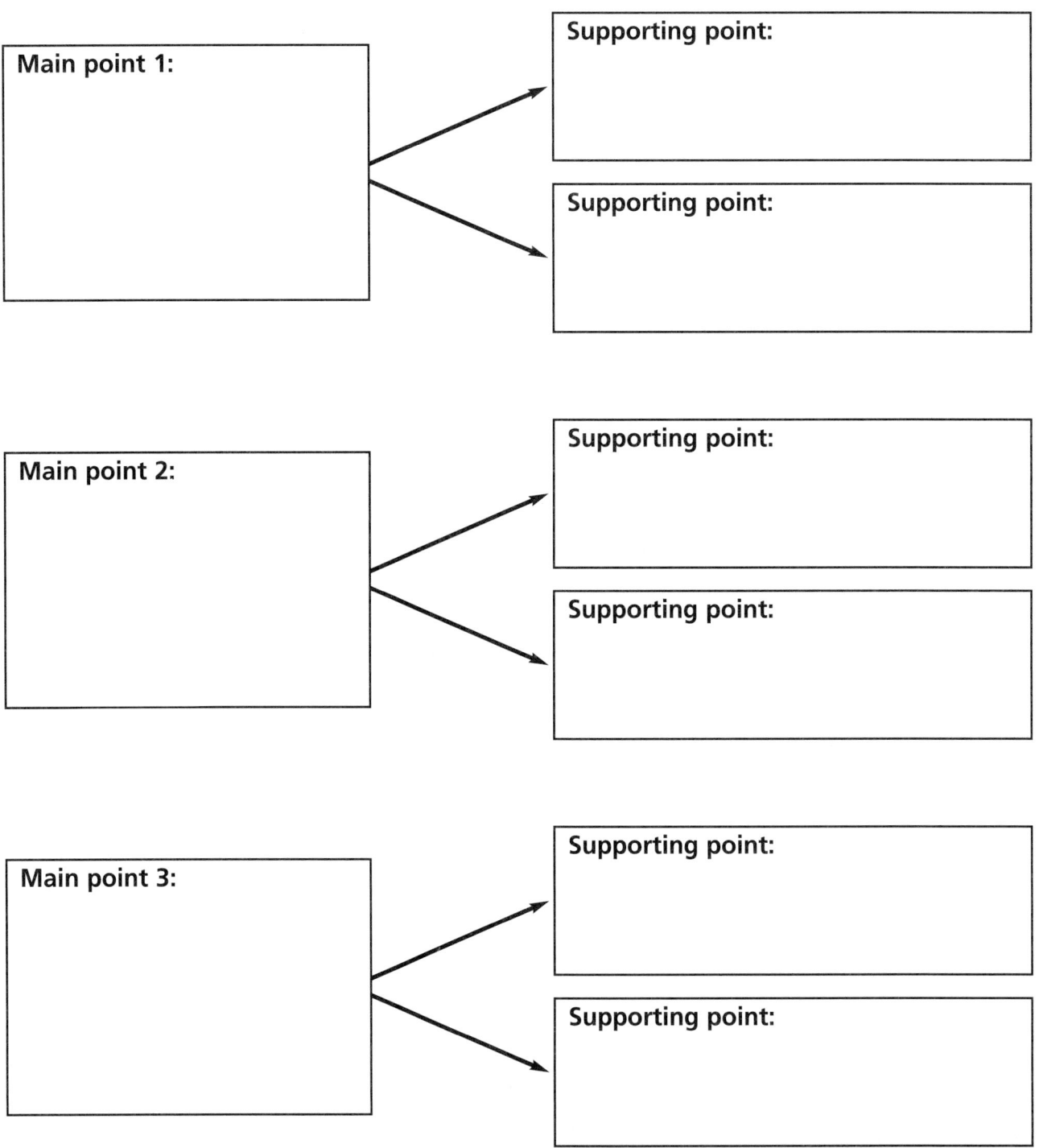

Unit 7 New media

OHT 7.8: Raising the level

Assessment Focus

AF2: Produce texts which are appropriate to task, reader and purpose

Level 3

The Internet allows people to get huge amounts of information. Not all of this is needed, you have to learn how to use search engines. John O'Farrell argues that the Internet is a waste of time, but it isn't if you learn to use search engines properly. You can also access all this information very fast.

Level 4

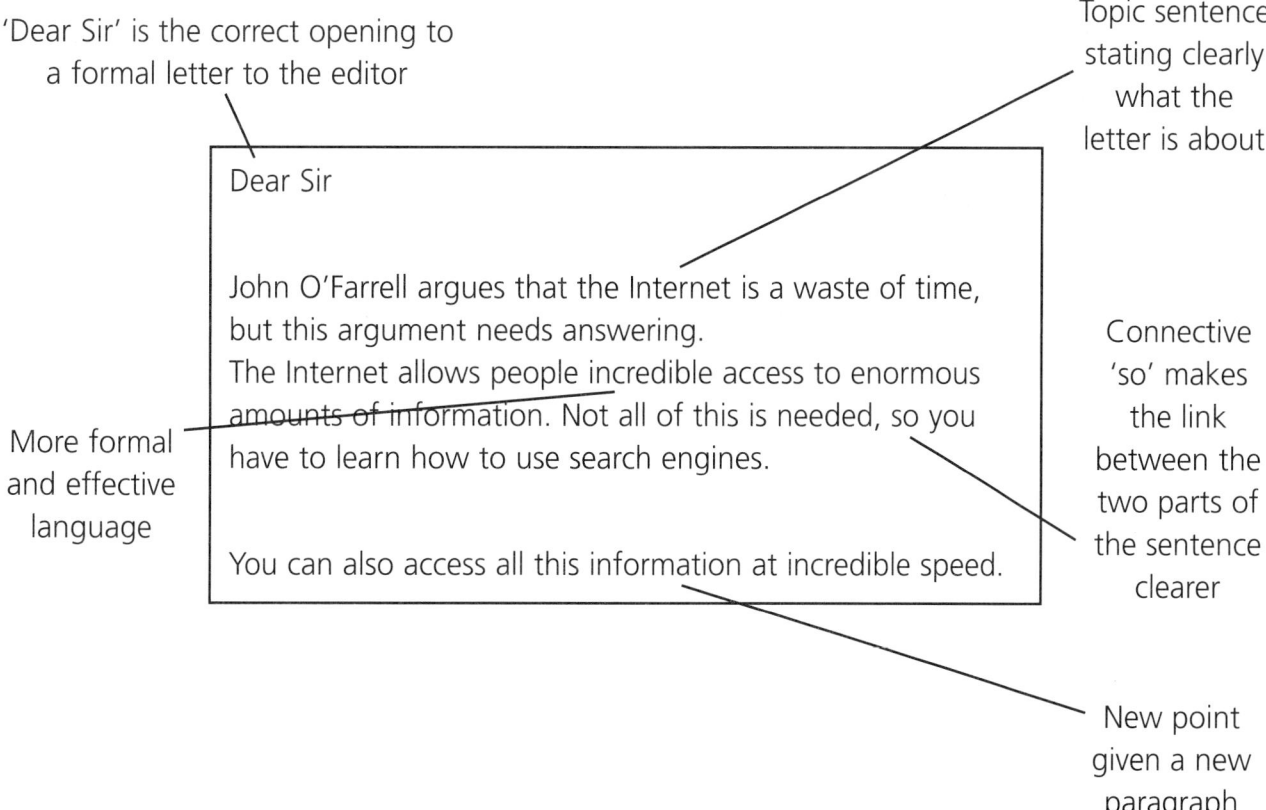

'Dear Sir' is the correct opening to a formal letter to the editor

Topic sentence stating clearly what the letter is about

Dear Sir

John O'Farrell argues that the Internet is a waste of time, but this argument needs answering.
The Internet allows people incredible access to enormous amounts of information. Not all of this is needed, so you have to learn how to use search engines.

You can also access all this information at incredible speed.

More formal and effective language

Connective 'so' makes the link between the two parts of the sentence clearer

New point given a new paragraph

Impact English Teacher's Resource © HarperCollinsPublishers 2005

Unit 8

Voices from the past

Lesson 1

Framework Objective

W2: Revise and remember high-frequency spellings
Main text type: Narrative

Student Book pages 166–169

Starter

- Dictate the following ten words from the narrative extract in the Student Book. They all include the vowel sound 'ay'. Students must write them down with the correct spelling:
  - *breaking*
  - *straight*
  - *snaking*
  - *again*
  - *away*
  - *late.*
  - *trained*
  - *face*
  - *bayonets*
  - *praying*
- Then check the spelling. Point out the different letter strings that show the same sound and write them on the board. Ask students whether they can think of any other words that include the sound 'ay' but use a different letter string (for example, *reign, grey, able, fête*).

Introduction

- Read through the Michael Morpurgo extract with the class, checking that glossary words are understood. Ask 1 or 2 students to describe what the story is about, referring to question **1**.

Key Reading

- Go through the key features of narrative texts as described in the text-type box on page 168. Check students' understanding by asking:
  - *What is the purpose of the 'development' section of any story (or episode)?*
  - *What does the term 'expressive' mean?*
  - *How do you know that the first-person narrator is one of the characters?*
- Students discuss questions **2**, **3** and **4** in pairs. You may need to offer guidance in question **3b** on the word classes that make the description effective. Ask 2 or 3 pairs to feed back their answers and invite the class to comment.

Development

Purpose

- Students discuss question **5** in small groups and feed back, providing evidence from the text to support their choice.

Reading for meaning

- Students answer questions **6** to **9**, working on their own or in pairs, then feed back. Students may need some support with question **8b**, which asks them to describe the effect of using a string of present participles ('–ing' verbs) to emulate the continuous movement of the gas itself.
- As an extension to question **9b** (or for homework), provide students with a copy of **Worksheet 8.1**. This offers a storyboard template on which to plan a film version of the extract. Remind students to include details of the dialogue and soundtrack in the caption boxes, and some simple indications of different camera shots that might be used (whether it is a long shot or a close-up).

Plenary

- Ask 2 or 3 students to present their storyboards to the class. Invite the class to comment on whether each storyboard adds to (or omits from) the written version.

Unit 8 Voices from the past

Worksheet 8.1: Storyboard

Use the template below to storyboard a film version of the *Private Peaceful* extract. For each frame:
- Draw a sketch (in the top box) to show what appears on-screen.
- Add key information (in the box underneath). For example, to describe the type of camera shot (long shot or close-up) and the soundtrack.

The first frame has already been completed to start you off.

Frame 1

Long shot of trench. Only sounds are quiet conversation and birdsong.

Frame 2

Frame 3

Frame 4

Frame 5

Frame 6

Impact English Teacher's Resource © HarperCollins Publishers 2005

Voices from the past

Framework Objectives
W11: Appreciate the impact of figurative language in texts
Wr5: Develop the use of commentary and description in narrative
Main text type: Narrative

Student Book pages 170–171

Starter

- Put this sentence on the board: *The cavalry moved across the plain towards the enemy.* Get students to brainstorm different ways in which this description can be made more interesting/effective, either by adding detail or changing words. This can be done in groups first, or as a whole-class activity throughout. Add suggestions to the sentence on the board, using key lines (as in a spidergram). Underline any that use imagery of different kinds. Ask for some images if students are not supplying any. Finally, write out one or two of the most effective new versions and compare them with the original. Make sure these include imagery.

Introduction

Focus on: Imagery

- Read through the section, emphasising the two main ingredients of effective imagery: powerful words and imaginative comparison. Highlight to students how these ingredients are present in the annotated example. Pairs then attempt question **10**, as modelled in the table on page 170 of the Student Book.
- To support question **10**, hand out a copy of **Worksheet 8.2** to each pair and ask them to complete the table. The main images are provided in column 1 of the table, so that students can concentrate on the analysis. Ask 2 or 3 pairs to present their tables and invite the class to comment.
- Question **11**, which touches on the personification of gas, could be covered during the feedback session for question **10**. Alternatively, you could ask students to locate the examples while completing their tables.

Development

Key Writing

- For question **12**, students write an imaginative story from the point of view of a German soldier first witnessing the use of tanks in battle in 1916. It may help to first provide students with more of an historical context; for example, by reading an historical description of an early tank attack to the class. (A good website on this is www.firstworldwar.com/battles/flers.htm). Drawing from the extract, historical sources and any other images available, pairs then brainstorm powerful words for their description before drafting their paragraphs individually. The same pairs peer review their first attempts and then redraft.

Plenary

- Ask 1 or 2 pairs to read out their descriptions to the class. Each pair should then state how their partner helped them to improve their draft. The rest of the class comment on the effectiveness of the descriptions, concentrating especially on the imagery.

Unit 8 Voices from the past

Worksheet 8.2: Imagery

In pairs, complete the table below by:
- in the second column, listing the powerful words used and their effect
- in the third column, identifying what the gas is being compared with and commenting on the effect of the comparison.

Description of gas from text (imagery)	Powerful words and effect	Comparison and effect
'…we see it rolling towards us, this dreaded killer cloud…'	rolling – like something mechanical dreaded – like…	a cloud – something large and threatening
'Its deadly tendrils are searching ahead… searching for me'		

Impact English Teacher's Resource © HarperCollins Publishers 2005

Framework Objective

S4: Explore the effects of changes in tense
Main text type: Discursive

Student Book pages 172–176

Starter

- Write four sentences on the board that use the simple present tense and four sentences that use the simple past. Use only regular verbs, i.e. those that form the past by adding '–ed' or '–d'. Ask pairs to identify the verbs and write them under the columns 'Present tense' and 'Past tense'. Invite feedback at this stage, to check that all students understand the distinction. Then ask pairs to change the present tenses to the past tense and vice versa. Finally, challenge students to work out the rule for forming the past tense of regular verbs.

Introduction

- Read through the extract with the class, checking that glossary words are understood. Ask 1 or 2 students to summarise what the text is about.

Key Reading

- Go through the key features of discursive texts as described in the text-type box on page 174. Check understanding by asking students:
  - *What would you expect to find in the conclusion of a discursive text?*
  - *Give an example of a signposting phrase.*
  - *What does 'tentative' mean?*
- Students discuss questions **1** to **5** in pairs. Invite 2 or 3 pairs to feed back their answers and invite the class to comment.
- More able students could annotate a section of the Mary Celeste text on **Worksheet 8.3**, to bring out examples of the main features of discursive texts. Ask 2 or 3 students to present their findings to the class as an OHT.

Development

Purpose

- In question **6**, students discuss the main purpose of the text in small groups. They should provide evidence from the text to support their choice. In the feedback session, encourage groups to consider what other purpose(s) the text might have.

Reading for meaning

- Pairs discuss questions **7**, **8** and **9**, which deal with the structure of the *Mary Celeste* text. For question **8**, it may help students to first run through the reasons why the present tense is often used in discursive texts. This will enable pairs to draw a contrast with the reasons why this text uses the past tense at certain points. Pairs then feed back with their answers.

Plenary

- Elicit from students the four key features of discursive texts; they should not refer to their textbooks.

Unit 8 — Voices from the past

Worksheet 8.3: Discursive texts

In the extract from the *Mary Celeste* article below, highlight at least **two** examples of each of the three main features of discursive texts:

- A **form** consisting of a series of points supported by **detail and evidence**
- **Phrases at the start of sentences**, to introduce a viewpoint
- **Tentative language**, to help express a range of possibilities.

If possible, use a different colour to highlight each feature.

Were the missing crewmen kippered by a squid?

In 1904 a magazine article claimed that the entire ship's company had been abducted by a giant octopus! According to the article, the well-armed creature rose from the deep and grabbed the ship's helmsman. The helmsman's yells brought the rest of the crew up on deck and, one by one, the octopus swept them up.

But could this have been what happened? Well, giant squid can be 20m (60ft) long, with eyes the size of a human head. But if a monster squid is the answer to the riddle, why did all hands remain on deck long enough to be plucked off in turn? And why did the squid make off with the ship's logbook, papers and lifeboat?

Did plundering pirates kill Captain Briggs and his crew?

Some people have suggested that pirates murdered Captain Briggs, his family and crew. But if pirates were to blame, where were the traces of violence you'd expect to see after a raid? And if sea-robbers had swarmed aboard the Mary Celeste, why hadn't they looted the ship from stem to stern? Amongst the things found on board were a silver watch, a fancy sword, some gold jewellery and expensive clothes.

Unit 8
Voices from the past
Lesson 4

Framework Objectives

S5: Recognise and exploit the use of conditionals and modal verbs when speculating, hypothesising or discussing possibilities

Wr16: Weigh different viewpoints and present a balanced analysis of an event or issue

Main text type: Discursive

Student Book pages 176–177

Starter

- Invite students in pairs to develop a short role-play in which they are two parents discussing where their son/daughter is. Each pair then gets together with another pair and listens carefully to the other's role-play. Ask students to jot down all the words and phrases that suggest possibility rather than fact. Give an example on the board first; for example: *I wonder if she is at Anna's house*; *Maybe he is at the park*.
- Once they have finished, ask several pairs to feed back their list of words and phrases that suggest possibility, and write them on the board. Elicit from the class any patterns or similarities in the words. Avoid using terms like 'modals' or 'conditionals' at this stage, but explain that students will refer to this work later.

Introduction

Focus on: The language of possibility

- Read through the section on the language of possibility with the class, ensuring that students understand the difference between a fact and a theory. If necessary, revisit the meaning of the term 'tentative'. Ask students to supply other examples of the three bulleted categories of tentative language on page 176, drawing on their role-play during the Starter.
- Pairs then attempt question **10**, using their copies of **Worksheet 8.3** from the last lesson. Students can write the factual versions of each example in the margin or on the back of the worksheet. Ask 2 or 3 pairs to present their responses to the class.

Development

Key Writing

- Read through question **11** with the class, answering any queries about the task. Then provide each student with the writing frame on **Worksheet 8.4**. Work with a group of students, sharing ideas for effective ways of using the language of possibility to question the theory. Showcase any particularly good sentences.

Plenary

- Ask 3 or 4 students to read out their paragraphs and ask the class to identify examples of tentative language. Finally, ask students to write down a sentence summarising how this lesson has helped them to write a discursive text.

Unit 8 Voices from the past

Worksheet 8.4: Assessing a theory

Here is another theory about the *Mary Celeste*. Use the writing frame below to compose a paragraph in the style of the main extract.

> **Theory:** Captain Briggs went mad and murdered his family and crew before throwing himself into the sea.
>
> **Points for:**
> It must have been stressful, being cooped up on a small ship.
> Such an event actually happened in 1828.
>
> **Points against:**
> He was a very experienced captain.
> The ship's lifeboat and logbook were also missing.

1 Give your paragraph a heading. Can you make it a question?

_____

2 Introduce the theory here. Use a phrase like 'Another theory is…' or 'Some people think…'

_____
_____
_____
_____

3 Describe the evidence for the theory. Include tentative words and phrases, such as 'could' and 'perhaps'.

_____
_____
_____
_____

4 Now describe the evidence against the theory.

_____
_____
_____
_____

Impact English Teacher's Resource © HarperCollins Publishers 2005

Unit 8
Voices from the past
Lesson 5

Framework Objective

Wr6: Experiment with figurative language in conveying a sense of character and setting

Main text type: Poetry

Student Book pages 178–181

Starter

- Ask the class what the difference is between rhythm and rhyme (two terms commonly confused at this level). Read the start of three or four different types of poem – choose those with strong rhythms and rhymes, for example, limericks, but include one in free verse. Ask the class to note down which have a regular rhythm, and which rhyme. Finally ask them to spell the two words – show on the board how each begins with 'rhy'.

Introduction

- Read the poem aloud to the class, checking that glossary words are understood. To enforce a basic understanding, ask students to answer question **1**.

Key Reading

- Go through the key features of poetry as shown in the text-type box on page 179. Check students' understanding by asking:
  - *A limerick is a type of poem. What pattern do its lines make?*
  - *Do all poems have a regular rhythm or beat?*
  - *Can there be different kinds of rhyme in a poem?*
- Students discuss questions **2** to **5** in pairs. Ask 2 or 3 pairs to feed back their answers and invite the class to comment. Ask students to make notes of the main points about the poem, to refer to when preparing their presentations for question **12**.

Development

Purpose

- Pairs discuss the main purpose of *Roman Wall Blues* in question **6**, providing evidence from the poem to support their choice.

Reading for meaning

- Students attempt questions **7** and **8** on their own and questions **9** and **10** in pairs. **Worksheet 8.5** provides an accessible method of tackling question **9**. This is the most important question, since it requires students to show understanding of every couplet in the poem. Refer students back to the work they did in the starter activity to help them with question **10**. Ask for feedback on all the questions before moving on.

Plenary

- Write out the first couplet of the poem on the board. Ask students to write a prose version that says much the same thing; they could write it as a sentence from a history book about Roman Britain, for example. Ask 2 or 3 students to read out their prose versions, then brainstorm with the class the main elements that make the poem different to the prose versions.

Unit 8 — Voices from the past

Worksheet 8.5: A soldier's daydreams

Trace the soldier's daydreams as he stands on sentry duty. Cut out the thoughts and feelings at the bottom of the page. Then decide which part of the poem each one relates to. Put it next to the relevant line or lines.

Roman Wall Blues

Over the heather the wet wind blows,
I've lice in my tunic and a cold in my nose.
The rain comes pattering out of the sky,
I'm a Wall soldier, I don't know why.
The mist creeps over the hard grey stone,
My girl's in Tungria; I sleep alone.
Aulus goes hanging around her place,
I don't like his manners, I don't like his face.
Piso's a Christian, he worships a fish;
There'd be no kissing if he had his wish.
She gave me a ring but I diced it away;
I want my girl and I want my pay.
When I'm a veteran with only one eye
I shall do nothing but look at the sky.

I bet other men are going after my girl – I hate them.	I wish my girlfriend was here – I miss her.
I'm broke and miserable on my own.	I'm cold, wet and uncomfortable.
I wish I hadn't gambled my girl's present away.	What on earth am I doing here?
I'm looking forward to when I retire.	

Impact English Teacher's Resource © HarperCollinsPublishers 2005

Voices from the past

Lesson 6

Framework Objectives

Wr17: Integrate evidence into writing to support analysis or conclusions (quotation)
S&L3: Make a formal presentation in standard English, using appropriate rhetorical devices
Main text type: Poetry

Student Book pages 182–183

Starter

- Explain that students will be giving a presentation at the end of the lesson. Brainstorm good points of advice to bear in mind when giving an oral presentation in front of an audience. (Cover ways of making voice interesting/audible; preparation; use of prompts; conquering nerves; body language – give these categories as prompts if necessary.)
- Write key points on the board, then ask groups to discuss which would be chosen as their top five key points for giving presentations.

Introduction

Focus on: Using quotations

- Read through the explanation, showing students how to integrate evidence into the analysis of a text. Model how each of the three bullet-pointed 'rules' on page 182 is followed up in the annotated example. Emphasise to students that they need to remember to do their PE (Point + Evidence) when they quote from a text. You could also give them this example of how not to do PE and invite comment on what is wrong with it:

  The poet says the mist creeps over the hard grey stone, My girl's in Tungria; I sleep alone, which shows how he is thinking about his girlfriend. He wants to be with her, but she is in Italy.

- Students answer question **11** in pairs. If they are stuck for ideas, point them to their answers to questions **5** and **10**. Ask 3 or 4 pairs to present their writing and invite the class to comment on how effectively each pair has made their points and backed them up with evidence from the poem.

Development

Key Speaking and Listening

- In question **12**, pairs prepare an analytical presentation of the poem *Roman Wall Blues*, following the guidance supplied on page 183 of the Student Book. Give each pair a copy of **Worksheet 8.6** to help them write their notes. Work with pairs to help them organise their thoughts, write notes and practise their presentations. Students can use an OHT of **Worksheet 8.5** to point to individual lines when they come to do their presentations.

Plenary

- Ask students to write down one thing they like about the poem and one thing they dislike about it. They should write full sentences and include evidence from the poem. Ask 3 or 4 students to read out their sentences.

Unit 8 Voices from the past

Worksheet 8.6: Presenting a poem

Complete the chart below with your notes on *Roman Wall Blues*. Use these notes when giving your presentation.

The subject of the poem What is the poem about? Who is the main character? Where and when is it set? From whose point of view is it written?	
The form or structure of the poem How is the poem laid out? Is there a special name for this form? Do the sentences follow any pattern?	
Rhythm and rhyme What kind of rhythm does the poem have? Is there a rhyme scheme – what is it? What effect do the rhythm and rhyme have? Are any other sound effects used in this poem?	

Voices from the past

Lesson 7

Assessment Focus
AF1: Write imaginative, interesting and thoughtful texts
Main text type: Poetry

Student Book pages 184–185

Starter

- Brainstorm with the class any facts or anecdotes they know about the D-Day landings; if possible, show a short clip from one of the many TV documentaries of recent years. Ask students to think about 'the ordinary person' involved in these events. How do they think a young soldier about to take part in such a momentous event felt and saw things?

Introduction

Stage 1

- Now bring more focus to the discussion by reading through the D-Day facts on page 184. Ask pairs to discuss the image for a few minutes, then jot down any ideas or impressions they develop about D-Day.

Stage 2

- Students brainstorm the thoughts and ideas of their character, working in the same pairs. To model how to do this, go over the spidergram on page 185 of the Student Book. You may also want to do a class rereading of Auden's *Roman Wall Blues*, as a model for portraying a character's thoughts and feelings honestly.

Development

Stage 3

- Read through the bullet point reminders with the class. Students then work on their own to produce their first drafts. Emphasise that they are only writing three or four rhyming couplets, so they will need to choose their best ideas and images. **OHT 8.7** provides an example of how to approach writing a first draft, to make the task less daunting.

Challenge

- Encourage those students with the time or ability to use more sound effects, such as alliteration, in their poem.

Peer Assessment

- When students have completed their poems, put them in pairs to read each other's drafts. Write up the following text-type features and ask students to check whether their drafts include them:
  - an imaginative picture of the character's thoughts and feelings
  - a regular form – lines grouped in couplets
  - a regular rhythm or beat
  - rhyme (and other sound effects).
- Students complete the Peer Assessment Sheet (see page 6) and feed back.
- Students redraft their poems according to suggestions.

Plenary

- Give a copy of **OHT 8.8** (top half only) to each pair and get students to annotate level 3 to show how well the student has incorporated the various features of poetry (images, rhythm, form) and what needs improvement. Then display the whole of **OHT 8.8** and ask for feedback on how to get the level 3 writing up to level 4. Show in the exemplar of level 4 how this can be done. Students then make changes to their own texts in light of this.
- Encourage students to read their poems aloud to the class.

Unit 8 Voices from the past

OHT 8.7: Drafting a poem

Follow the steps in this flowchart to help you draft your poem.

Step 1 Your first draft

Choose one of the ideas in your spidergram. Write two lines about it that rhyme and have a strong rhythm. Don't expect it to be perfect at this stage!

> The sky is full of lead
> And I just want to be in bed.

Step 2 Checking the rhyme

Make sure your couplet rhymes, as this one does. If you can't think of a rhyme for a particular word, try ending the first line with a simpler word. 'Ill' is easier to rhyme than 'seasick'!

> I'm feeling rather ~~seasick~~ *ill*
> I don't want to kill.

Step 3 Checking the rhythm

If you're having trouble with the rhythm, try reading the verse out loud. You could also clap the rhythm. Count the beats to make sure you have the same number in each line.

> The sky is / *getting* full of lead
> And I just want to be in bed.

Step 4 Revising your draft

Look over the poem carefully when you have finished.
- Can you make any words or images more powerful? (Make sure you don't upset the rhythm or rhyme when you revise.)

> The sky is / *filling up with* ~~getting full of~~ lead
> And I just want to be in bed.

Unit 8 Voices from the past

OHT 8.8: Raising the level

Assessment Focus

AF1: Write imaginative, interesting and thoughtful texts

Level 3

The fishes swimming on the sea bed
I don't want them to eat me when I'm full of led

I'd like to live a good long life
I really don't want to die here

Level 4

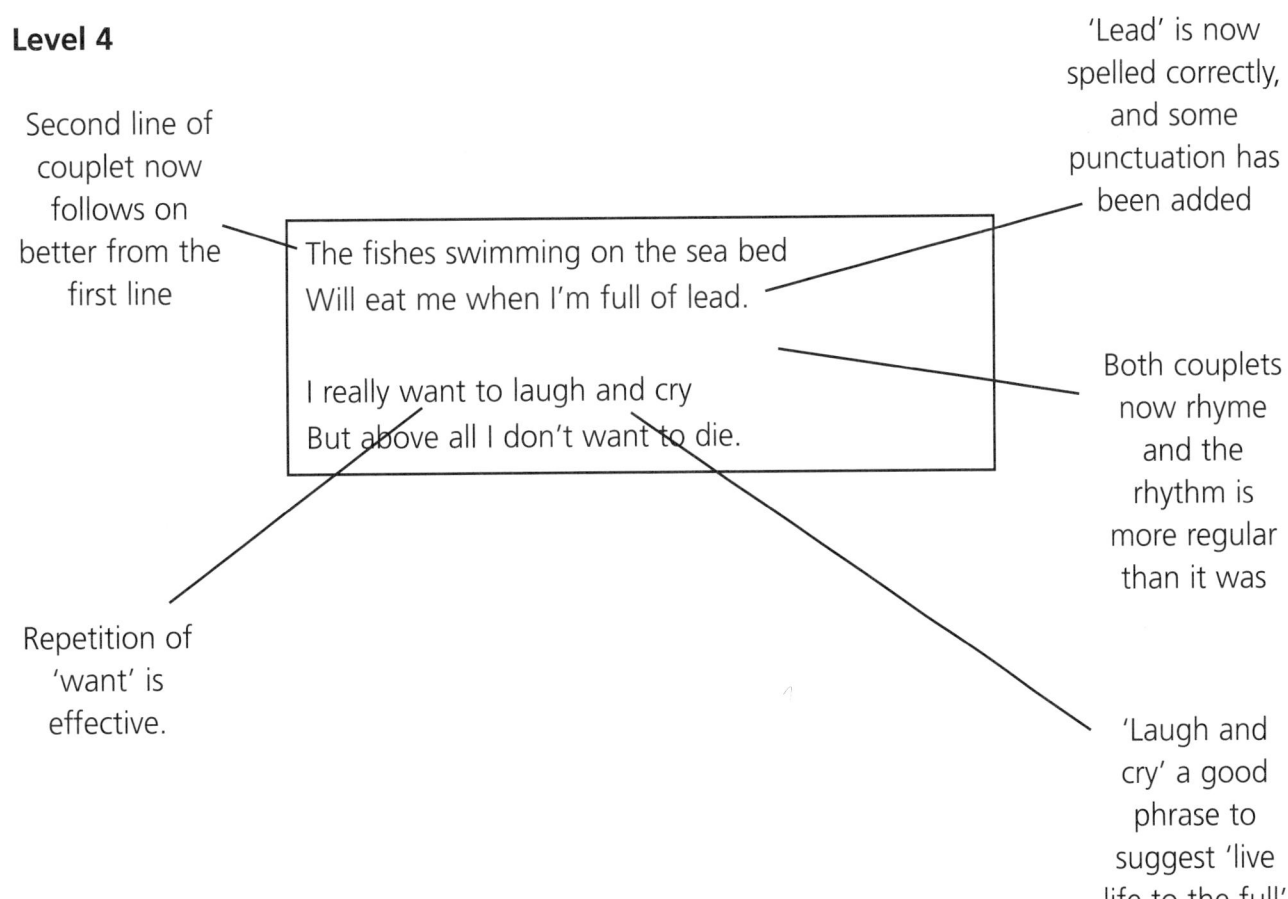

Impact English Teacher's Resource © HarperCollins Publishers 2005

Unit 9
Dangerous pursuits
Lesson 1

Framework Objective
W1d: Review, consolidate and secure conventions (prefixes)
Main text type: Information

Student Book pages 186–189

Starter

- Build up a family of words/spellings on the board around the word 'extreme' – for example: *extremist, extremity, extremism, extremely*.
- Ask students to identify the different functions of the words (nouns and adverb). Ask students whether they know what the prefix 'ex–' means. ('Ex' = 'out of' or 'on the outside'.) Why is this meaning appropriate for an 'extremist'?
- The prefix 'im–' also changes the meaning of the root word it is attached to (for example, '*im*possible', '*im*practical'). What do students think it means?

Introduction

- Read through the text with students, checking that glossary words are understood. Ask 1 or 2 students to describe what the text is about.

Key Reading

- Go through the key features of information texts as described in the text-type box on page 188. Check students' understanding of the text-type features and how they apply to this text by asking:
  - *How is this text similar to the sort of text you would get in an encyclopaedia or other reference book?*
- Pairs work through questions **1** to **4** then feed back to the class. Support students in distinguishing between the impersonal language of most of the text and the chatty words and phrases discussed in question **4**.

Development

Purpose

- Draw the table in question **5** on the board and work through the responses with the class, asking students to contribute evidence to the table. Make sure that students are quite precise about the evidence they find.

Reading for meaning

- In order to answer question **6**, students should search for the key words to identify the three different sections (equipment and clubs; what extreme sports are; how extreme sports can help people's bodies). Ask students to scan the text looking for the key word(s), then check to see whether the reference is relevant.
- Then ask students whether they know what 'adrenalin' is; if they do not, look it up in a dictionary before answering question **7**.
- Draw attention to, or write on the board, the following sentence from the text:
  Regular extreme sports thrills can result in improved well being, less stress and more confidence.
  Ask the class what they notice about the 'number pattern' of this sentence. The answer is that it is a 'pattern of three', which is often used when explaining the benefits of something (particularly in persuasive speeches).
- To expand on this work, display **OHT 9.1**. Model the first two examples of the 'pattern of three' then complete the third example with the class. You can draw attention to the other features (alliteration and repetition) if you wish, though these do not feature in the *Extreme Sport* text. Students attempt examples 4 and 5 working on their own.

Plenary

- Ask 3 or 4 students to feed back their responses to examples 4 and 5 on **OHT 9.1**. Record their answers on the board and invite the class to comment.

Unit 9 Dangerous pursuits

OHT 9.1: Patterns of three

Example 1

The new Estra is sporty, stylish and sexy!

Example 2

A vote for us is a vote for strong government, strong leadership and a strong country!

Example 3

Come to the party! There'll be great music, _____ and _____.

Example 4

Fruit is cheap, _____ and _____.

Example 5

Going on holiday relaxes you, _____ you _____ and _____.

Dangerous pursuits

Framework Objectives

S10: Identify the key alterations made to a text when it is changed from an informal to a formal text

S12: Explore and use different degrees of formality in written and oral texts

Main text type: Information

Student Book pages 190–191

Starter

- Write the following text on the board or read it sentence by sentence:
  'I was *down* the pub having a lemonade when the landlord told me my *missus* was on the *blower*. So I *goes* over and spoke to her. She was *doing her nut cos* I was meant to pick the *kids* up from some *do* at the school. So, I had to *leg it sharpish* and get over there as soon as I could.'
- Ask students to 'translate' this (very) informal text. There is no need to make it especially formal; students should simply change the selected (italicised) words and phrases. Write alternative words and phrases on the board and ask the class to decide on the best choices.

Introduction

Focus on: Informal and formal texts

- Stress that formality is all about suitability – sometimes it is appropriate to speak or write in a chatty, informal way; on other occasions, this would be out of place. Complete question **8** as a class and ask students to identify the informal aspects of the text and decide what has been changed. Then work through the examples in question **9**, asking students to think of suitable alternatives. If students seem confident, this activity can be done in pairs, with students feeding back their alternative words and phrases.

Development

Key Writing

- Introduce question **10** and read through the text about climbing. You may want to model the first change for the class before students attempt the task on their own.
- Distribute **Worksheet 9.2** to students so that they do not have to rewrite the whole text. This also suggests possible replacement words and phrases. Encourage students to try these out in pencil first, so they can alter them if they wish. You may want to guide a particular group of students in making their choices.

Plenary

- Ask 3 or 4 students to share their rewritten texts from question **10**, then ask the class the following questions:
  – *Were there any changes they found especially difficult?*
  – *What is the effect of making the text more formal?*
  – *Does it seem as though it is intended for a different audience?*
- You might want to comment on the fact that a simile (*I feel like a million dollars*), albeit a clichéd one, is likely to have been replaced by a simple adjective (such as 'brilliant' or 'fantastic'). Ask students whether the language is less colourful in the formal version.

Unit 9 — Dangerous pursuits

Worksheet 9.2: Informal climbing

Read the following extract from the *Extreme Sport* text:

> Climbing is a well-cool thing to do. When I'm perched on top of some peak, I feel like a million dollars, but you don't get there by luck.
>
> You gotta get real. If you wanna get a buzz out of it, you need to do it safely.
>
> You'll need the proper stuff – and the right guys around you. It's no use being surrounded by your mates who have never seen a mountain in their lives.
>
> Nah. I reckon you need expert help. Dudes who know what they're blabbin' on about.

Now look at the version of the extract below. The informal words and phrases have been removed.

> Climbing is a _____ to do. When I'm perched on top of some peak, I feel _____, but you don't get there by luck.
>
> You _____. If you _____ get a _____ out of it, you need to do it safely.
>
> You'll need the proper _____ – and the right _____ around you. It's no use being surrounded by your _____ who have never seen a mountain in their lives.
>
> _____. I _____ you need expert help. _____ who know what they're _____.

Replace the informal words and phrases with more formal words and expressions.

Below are some possible words for you to use. Be careful: not all of them will work!

- fantastic
- so proud
- must understand
- must face the facts
- want to
- have to

- thrill
- equipment
- singing about
- good feeling
- clothes
- children
- toys

- people
- wonderful
- brilliant
- no
- not
- not at all
- friends

- talking about
- food
- believe
- feel
- think.

Dangerous pursuits

Lesson

Framework Objectives

R4: Review their developing skills as active, critical readers who search for meaning using a range of reading strategies

S8: Know and use effectively the vocabulary, sentence grammar and stylistic conventions of the writing forms featured in specific subjects during the current year

Main text type: Explanation

Student Book pages 192–196

Starter

- Point out that certain words have special technical meanings but mean something slightly different when used in an everyday way. To illustrate this point, ask students how the word 'pressure' might be used differently in school subjects such as Science, Geography and Art. How is the same word often used in everyday life and the media?

Introduction

- Read through the text with students, checking that glossary words are understood. Ask 1 or 2 students to describe what the text is about.

Key Reading

- Go through the key features of information texts as described in the text-type box on page 194. Check students' understanding by asking:
  – In what school subjects would you be most likely to hear the language of cause and effect used in this way? (Science and Geography.)
  – Why is it natural to use the present tense in an explanation text, especially a spoken one?
- Students work through questions **1**, **2** and **3** in pairs. When pairs feed back their answers to question **2**, refer back to previous discussions on the use of causal language (and the fact that causal connectives help to highlight how or why something works or happens).

Development

Purpose

- Through question **4**, elicit the idea that the writer is instructing the reader how to *do* an experiment but that the experiment itself explains how *something happens*.
- Revisit imperatives and time connectives through the 'Grammar for reading' box on page 195 of the Student Book. Students then answer question **5** in pairs. When feeding back, ask them to point to the relevant references in the text. In question **6**, pairs identify the features of this explanation that make it a fun science text and not just a dry explanation.

Reading for meaning

- The focus of question **7** in highlighting the lack of complex science in the text is intended to get students thinking about its audience (probably non-science specialists or children).
- To help students visualise the changes they might make in question **8**, hand out copies of **Worksheet 9.3**. Students can work through the points on their own.

Plenary

- Ask students to feed back their design ideas from question **8**. It may be useful to use the text available on the accompanying CD-Rom text, to enable students to apply their ideas to a Word version of the article.

Unit 9 Dangerous pursuits

Worksheet 9.3: Designed to explain

Your task is to suggest design improvements for *The science of bungee-jumping* text. Here are some features you could include:

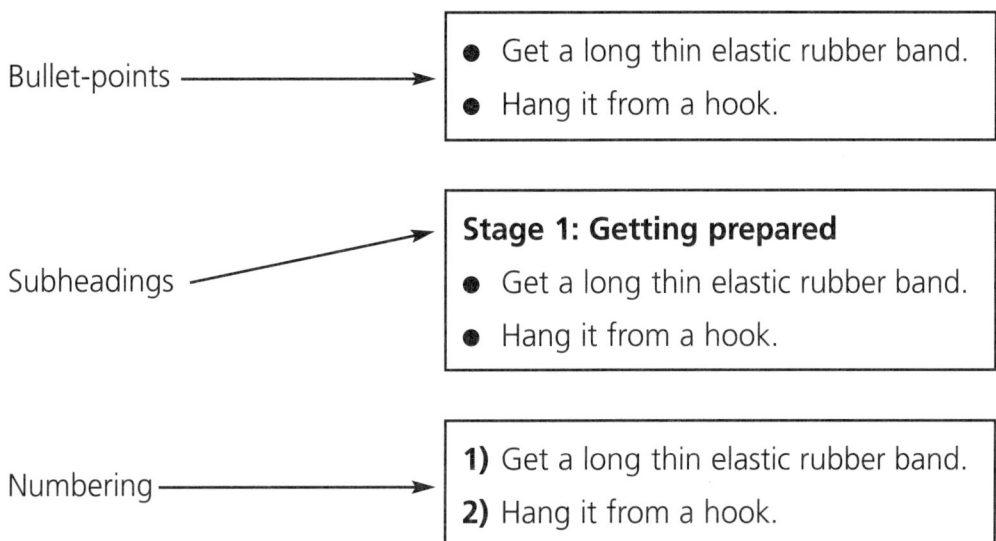

You could also include images and illustrations.

Firstly, I would make the layout better by _____
_____
_____
_____

Secondly, I would make it better by _____
_____
_____
_____

Use the other side of this sheet to plan how your new layout might look.

Unit 9
Dangerous pursuits
Lesson 4

Framework Objectives

S&L4: Provide an explanation or commentary which links words with actions or images

S&L5: Ask questions to clarify understanding and refine ideas

Main text type: Explanation

Student Book pages 197–198

Starter

- The following activity is designed to provide students with some practice in the range of questions that can be used to aid an explanation. First, give the class a quick speech about 'How I prepared before…' (for example, *an exam*, *a sports match*, *a wedding*, *a job interview* – whatever you choose). Invite students to ask you questions using 'why', 'when' and 'how', to draw out a fuller explanation.

Introduction

Focus on: Writing your own explanation or commentary

- If possible, show a short extract from a wildlife documentary; if not, read out the example on page 197 of the Student Book, to give a sense of the style of language used. Then ask pairs to take on the role of a wildlife presenter (Student A) and pretend to describe to the viewer (Student B) one of the following scenes:
  - *Lions sleeping then hunting down a gazelle.*
  - *A diver in a cage watching a killer shark circling.*
  - *Describing students in a classroom as though they are animals in a zoo (for example, Here we have the sleepy and slow-moving Leeus Smithus, a grumpy male who…)*
- Stress to students that it is the style of language they are trying to imitate which is important, not the accuracy of the explanation. Encourage them to speak in the present tense and, if possible, to use the language of cause and effect; however, this is not vital at this point. Each student should have a turn at being the wildlife presenter.
- Hand out **Worksheet 9.4** to each pair, as a prompt for the types of words and phrases the presenter might use. Run through these with the class, then move amongst pairs as they work, praising those students who adopt the right tone and register. Remind them that using 'we' is a common technique when sharing images and experiences on-screen.
- With the role play as preparation, students link the sentences in question **9**.

Development

Key Speaking and Listening

- In the same pairs, students look at the drawings for the 'Acid Drop' or 'Drop Off' at the start of question **10**. Explain that the key difference here is that whilst they will be giving a commentary, the important thing is to explain *how* it is done.
- Write these helpful explanatory phrases and links on the board:
  - *It's best to…because/as…*
  - *Try to…so that…*
  - *If you…then…*
- Next, model the example for the first picture on page 198.
- Students run through their commentaries in pairs, taking it in turns to be the 'expert skateboarder' and the listener. Encourage the listener to ask the expert a range of questions to clarify what is being said (*How…?, Why…?, So what you're saying is…*), reminding students of work previously done during the Starter.

Plenary

- Ask students to present a selection of their commentaries to the class, who then comment on the clarity of the explanation and the entertainment value. Point out examples where the style is particularly successful.

Unit 9 Dangerous pursuits

Worksheet 9.4: Animal language

Use the following words and phrases for your wildlife documentary, if you wish:

Introducing scenes and/or topics:	**Settings phrases:**
Here we have…	In the African bush…
Let's look at…	By a clump of trees…
If we look here, we can see…	Just beneath the ocean's surface…
We can find…	Behind that rock…
	Underneath that log…

Commenting:	**Drama/tension:**
This means…	But wait…
What we can see is…	Suddenly…
Why does this happen? Because…	Something seems to have…
As a result, you can see that…	We are just getting close when…
No one knows why…	It's time to…
It has been suggested that…	Disaster…
Perhaps…	

You can use the following box to note down some lines you might use. An example has already been done for you, to start you off.

If we look closely, under the ocean's surface, we can see the shadow of the Great White shark…

Dangerous pursuits

Framework Objective

R4: Review their developing skills as active, critical readers who search for meaning using a range of reading strategies

Main text type: Recount

Student Book pages 199–203

Starter

- Check that students are familiar with and understand the idea of actions in sentences having a clear tense ('I went') and also incomplete or non-tense related actions. Write the following sentences on the board and ask which *parts* of them can be said to be a continuous or incomplete action:
  – *Despite looking for ages, all I could find was my old passport.*
  – *I picked up the ring, wondering what she'd say.*
- There are other non-finite verb forms but this structure is appropriate for the recounts that students will read and write in this section.

Introduction

- Read the extract with students, checking that glossary words are understood. Then ask 1 or 2 students to describe what the text is about.

Key Reading

- Go through the key features of recount texts as described in the text-type box on page 201. Check students' understanding of the text-type features by asking:
  – In the second to last paragraph (lines 60–63), the writer uses two phrases related to time. What are they? ('for the moment' and 'after')
  – Can you find a powerful verb in paragraph 2 describing the movement of the snow?
- Pairs complete questions **1** to **4** in pairs to embed this knowledge. Ask 2 or 3 pairs to feed back and invite the class to comment.

Development

Purpose

- Elicit from students what would be lost if any one of the three bulleted features on page 202 (drama and tension, emotions, exact events) wasn't present in the text (it would be a very unemotional, factual report). Prepared in this way, pairs then discuss the options in question **5** before feeding back to the class.

Reading for meaning

- The purpose of question **6** is to show students how it is possible to draw conclusions from a text, whether things are said directly or implied (an idea they may have come across in other lessons). Students can work individually to match the boxes on page 203, but should be careful about linking the four pairs of boxes. Encourage them to focus on clues in the text that signal emotion (for example, the use of the exclamation mark can show anger, shock or emphasis, and is unlikely to be used when feeling 'not concerned'). During a feedback session, explore any differences in students' answers.

Plenary

- Conclude by working with the class to plot on **OHT 9.5** the changing feelings the writer shows in the first three paragraphs of the extract. Point out that these feelings can change *within* the paragraphs. If time allows, add further examples from the remainder of the text, which will include some of those from the matching exercise (question **6**).

Unit 9 Dangerous pursuits

OHT 9.5: Emotional rescue

Feelings/emotions	Quotations
Paragraph 1: Pleading, beginning to feel desperate. ⬇	'…to urge Joe…'
Paragraph 2: Beginning to feel scared, panic beginning to grow. ⬇	
Paragraph 3:	

Dangerous pursuits

Lesson 6

Framework Objectives

S1: Combine clauses into complex sentences, using the comma effectively as a boundary signpost and checking for fluency and clarity

S2: Explore the impact of a variety of sentence structures

Main text type: Recount

Student Book pages 203–205

Starter

- Read the following text aloud to the class:
  I stopped. Looked around. Was that footsteps? No. I must have been mistaken. But wait – what was that? It was footsteps! Getting closer. Closer every moment. Louder. Then louder still. Then they stopped. Silence. I could hear my heart beating like a drum.
- Ask students to:
  - guess how many sentences the extract contains
  - punctuate the section, from the start to 'It was footsteps!'.
- Point out that there are a number of 'non-sentences' here but that short sentences like this create the jumpy, nervy feel of the text.

Introduction

Focus on: Different sentence structures

- Begin question **7** by building on work done during the Starter. Look at the two examples on pages 203–204 and ask students to suggest why the first example is better.
- Next, go through the examples of sentences with non-finite clauses on page 204. You may choose not to use the term 'non-finite clause', but ensure that students understand the continuous nature of actions in these clauses. If reinforcement is needed, remind them of their work during the Starter for **Lesson 5**. Stress how useful this structure is in all writing but especially in narrative or recount texts. Finally, use question **8** to test students' knowledge; it may be best if they decide on the correct answer independently and then feed back.

Development

Key Writing

- Before students attempt question **9**, model the first example of a sentence containing a non-finite clause on **OHT 9.6**. Point out that the use of non-finite clauses allows the writer to cram more information into one sentence, and that this can add to the flow, the drama or the descriptive nature of a text. Then ask for contributions from the class to complete the remaining boxes on the OHT. If students need more assistance with this task, offer the following verbs from which additional clauses can be constructed.
  - Box 1: 'to stumble', 'to fall', 'to slip'
  - Box 2: 'to glance', 'to search', 'to check'
  - Box 3: 'to stop', 'to race', 'to skid'
  - Boxes 4 and 5 have already been completed, to round off the story and provide further reinforcement.
- Students then complete the three sentences in question **9** and devise two more of their own. Invite more confident students to add a further paragraph to the text, using additional non-finite clauses to provide further detail and drama.

Plenary

- Ask 3 or 4 students to share their examples of clauses constructed as part of question **9**. Invite the class to comment on how effectively they have used non-finite clauses to add tension and descriptive detail.

Unit 9: Dangerous Pursuits

OHT 9.6: Non-finite clauses

The failed robbery

Running for the car, the thief…
He stood up…
Its brakes screeching, an unmarked police-car…
Grabbing the man, *they searched and then arrested him*.
They took him away, *restraining him* in case he tried to escape.

Unit 9 Assignment

Unit 9
Dangerous pursuits

Lesson 7

Assessment Focus
AF4: Construct paragraphs and use cohesion within and between paragraphs
Main text type: Recount

Student Book pages 206–207

Starter

- Briefly revise the various functions of paragraphs, eliciting the following information from students:
  - they separate information – even if 'generally' related
  - they show a shift in time
  - they introduce new ideas or contrasting views
  - they elaborate on a previous idea.

Introduction

Stage 1

- Elicit background information for the task by asking students:
  - *Who was Captain Scott?*
  - *What was his goal or quest?*
  - *Was he successful?*
  - *What happened to him and his team?*
- Ensure that students understand they will be writing as an explorer in the present day, not from the 1900s (when Scott led his expedition). Also point out that students' written accounts should focus on one specific incident, as in the *Touching the Void* extract.
- Read through the explorer's notes about the incident and ask students to describe what has happened.

Stage 2

- Give out **Worksheet 9.7**, which supports students in dividing up their detailed notes and preparing a paragraph plan. More confident students may wish to break the notes into more than three paragraphs, depending on the amount of detail required. This is an alternative way of planning the paragraphs to using a timeline, as suggested on page 207 of the Student Book.

Development

Stage 3

- Students draft their first paragraph, keeping their plan in mind.

Peer Assessment

- Once students have finished their recounts, they work in pairs to read each other's drafts. Since this is only the first paragraph of their recount, some of the following text-type features may not be identified. However, write the following list on the board and ask students to check the drafts for:
  - some reference to time or the order of events
  - powerful, descriptive language
  - a variety of sentences.
- Students complete the Peer Assessment Sheet (see page 6) and feed back.
- Students then redraft according to suggestions and complete the remaining paragraphs.

Plenary

- Give a copy of **OHT 9.8** (top half only) to each group and get students to annotate the level 3 writing to show how well the student has used paragraphs and what needs improvement. Then display the whole of **OHT 9.8** and ask for feedback on how to get the level 3 writing up to level 4. Show in the exemplar of level 4 how this can be done. Students make changes to their own texts in light of this.

Unit 9 Dangerous pursuits

Worksheet 9.7: Planning paragraphs

Divide the following notes into three sections (each section will be a paragraph in your recount), using the table at the bottom of the page.

Each paragraph (section) should deal with a separate part of the story. The first paragraph has been highlighted for you, as an example.

Paragraph 1 →

Notes:
Day 24 Blizzard.
On the Beardmore Glacier.
Heading for the Ross Sea.
Temperature – 2 degrees Celsius.
Sam has fever, can't go on.
We pitch camp, and I call for assistance.
Weather so bad helicopter cannot find us or land.
We decide to try to get out of glacier before temperature drops any more.
I pull Sam on a sled behind me.
He's looking bad.
Stop and check satellite navigation system.
Isn't working. Can't go on.
Suddenly helicopter appears out of nowhere and lands. Saved!

Paragraph	Detail
Paragraph 1	Me walking through the snow; Sam behind me, then falling to the ground.
Paragraph 2	
Paragraph 3	

150 Impact English Teacher's Resource © HarperCollinsPublishers 2005

Unit 9 Dangerous pursuits

OHT 9.8: Raising the level

Assessment Focus

AF4: Construct paragraphs and use cohesion within and between paragraphs

Level 3

I turned and saw Sam on the ground looking really ill. I went over to him to see if he was ok, but he wasn't. Maybe he was dead I thought but then I saw he was breathing. I helped him stand up. We put the tent up and it was very difficult because of the strong blizzard. Eventually, we managed to get the tent up.

Level 4

Good variety of sentence starters

Individual details help paint picture

> Wiping the snow from my face, I turned and saw Sam, lying on the icy ground. I fought my way over to him. Was he ok? I couldn't tell when I clasped his arm. Yes, he was breathing. Clasping his arm, I helped him get to his feet.
>
> Putting the tent up was not easy. Sam tried to help, but it was impossible. He was just too weak. I thought – 'we're finished – we'll never get out.' However, Sam smiled and seemed to get some extra strength. Maybe, just maybe, we would make it.

New paragraph for new action

Connectives link sentences

More emotion – stronger word

Impact English Teacher's Resource © HarperCollinsPublishers 2005